# Sharks

Educational Poems

By

Nikki Hughey

For

Quintin

Acanthodian

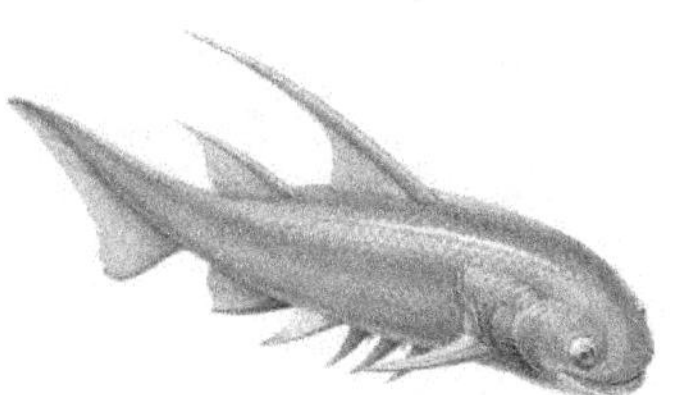

Hello I'm an acanthodian

I'm one of the first sharks

I lived two hundred ninety million years ago

I ate plankton

I could be up to thirty centimeters long

I had color vision

I had no teeth

African dwarf saw shark

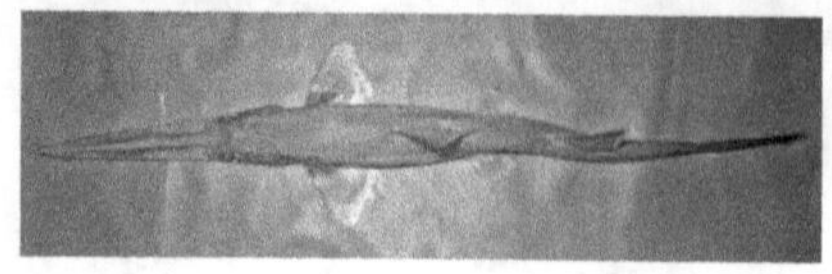

Hello I'm an African dwarf saw shark

I live in the Indian Ocean

I like deep water

I can be up to 61.6 centimeters long

My nose is one third of my total length

# Angel shark

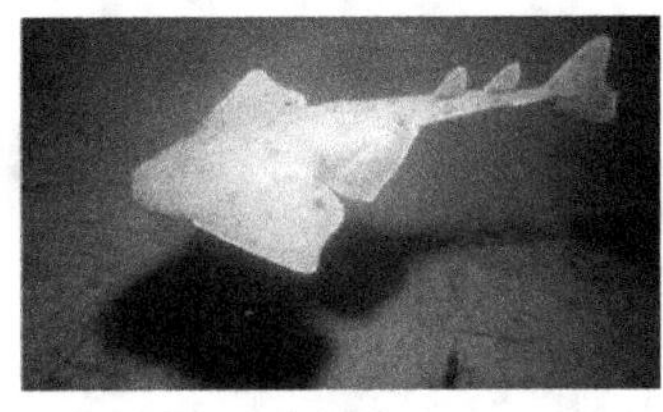

Hello I'm an angel shark

I have five gill slits

I can be up to 2.5 meters long

I live in warm water

Angular angel shark

Hello I'm an angular angel shark

I live in the Atlantic Ocean

I eat fish, crustaceans, and mollusk

I can be up to one hundred thirty centimeters long

I'm endangered

Angular rough

shark

Hello I'm an

angular rough shark

I can be up to a hundred centimeter long

I live in muddy water

In the Atlantic Ocean and the Mediterranean

I'm vulnerable

Arabian carpet shark

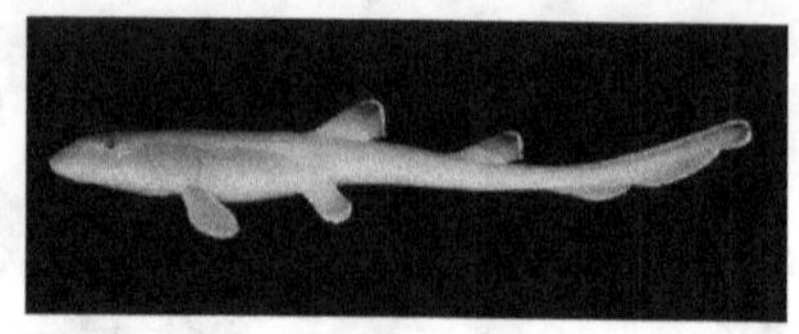

Hello I'm an Arabian carpet shark

I can be up to eighty centimeters long

I live in the Indian Ocean

I like mud, rocks, lagoons, reefs, shallow water, and mangroves

I eat eel, squid, crustaceans, and mollusk

Argentine angel shark

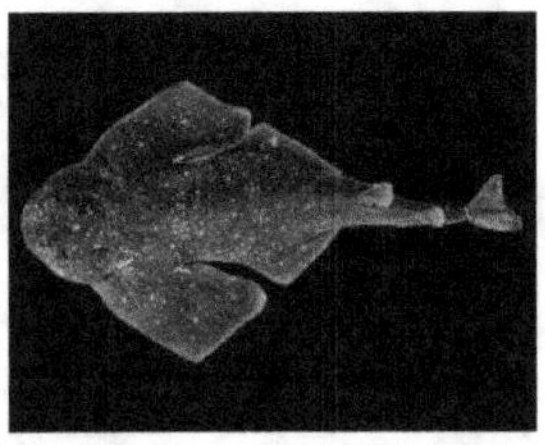

Hello I'm an Argentine angel shark

I live in the Atlantic Ocean

I can be up to one hundred seventy centimeters long

I'm endangered

I like mud, sand, and shallow water

I eat shrimp, squid, and fish

Atlantic ghost cat shark

Hello I'm an Atlantic ghost cat

shark

I like deep water

I eat fish and invertebrates

I live in the Atlantic Ocean

I can be more than twenty-five centimeters long

Atlantic weasel shark

Hello I'm an Atlantic weasel shark

I'm hunted for food and fish food

I live in the Atlantic Ocean

I can be up to one hundred thirty-eight centimeters long

I eat cephalopods and fish

I can have up to sixty-three teeth

Australian angel shark

Hello I'm an Australian angel

shark

I live in the Pacific and Indian Oceans

I like seagrass, rocks, and mud

I eat fish and crustaceans

I like sand

I can be up to one hundred fifty-two centimeters long

Australian black spotted

cat shark

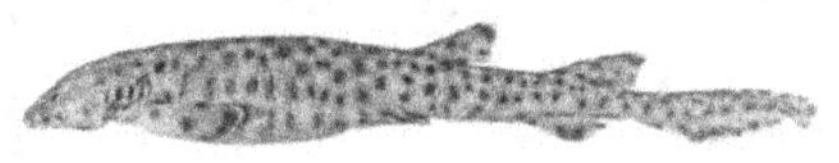

Hello I'm an Australian black spotted cat shark

I'm awake at night

I like shallow water

I live in the Indian Ocean

I can be up to sixty-seven centimeters long

Australian ghost shark

Hello I'm an Australian ghost

shark

I can be up to 1.5 meters long

I can live up to fifteen years

I live between Australia and New Zealand

I eat fish and invertebrates

I'm hunted for food

I'm a close relative of the elephant shark

Australian swell shark

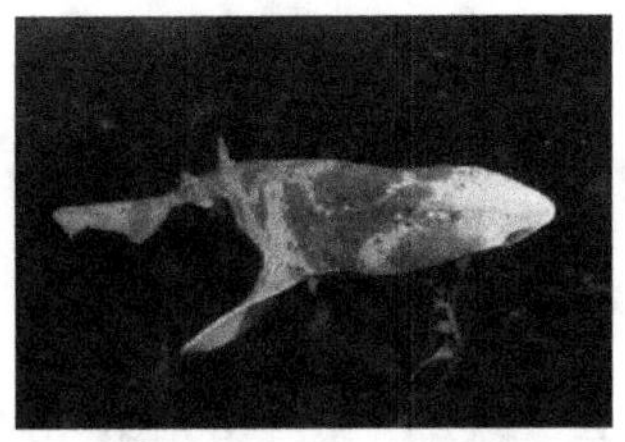

Hello I'm an Australian swell

shark

I like shallow water

I can be up to one hundred fifty centimeters long

I eat fish, squid, and crustaceans

If I'm afraid I inflate my belly with water or air

Australian weasel shark

Hello I'm an Australian weasel shark

I eat cephalopods

I like sand, seagrass and reefs

I live in the Pacific and Indian Oceans

I can be up to one hundred ten centimeters long

Balloon shark

Hello I'm a balloon shark

I live in the Indian Ocean

If I'm afraid I inflate myself with air or water

I like sand and mud

I eat crustaceans, fish, and cephalopods

I have one hundred fourteen teeth

I can be up to seventy-five centimeters long

Bamboo shark

Hello I'm a bamboo shark

I can be up to thirty-seven inches long

I'm hunted for food and medicine

I live in the Pacific and Indian Oceans

I like warm water and coral reefs

I'm awake at night

I eat invertebrates and fish

Banded cat shark

Hello I'm a banded cat shark

People keep me as a pet

I like sand, reefs, and tide pools

I eat krill, shrimp, squid, mussel, and clam

I live in the Indo-Pacific

I can be up to forty inches long

Banded hound shark

Hello I'm a banded hound shark

I live in the Pacific Ocean

I like sand, seaweed, and eelgrass

I can be up to one hundred fifty centimeters long

I eat invertebrates

I like to live alone

I'm awake at night

I can live up to eighteen years

I do well in captivity

Bandringa

Hello I'm a Bandringa

I could be up to three meters long

I lived in Illinois, Pennsylvania, and Ohio

I lived in fresh shallow water as an adult

I lived in salt water as a baby

I lived during the Moscovian

Barbel throat carpet shark

Hello I'm a barbel throat carpet shark

I live in the South China Sea

I can be up to thirty-four centimeters long

Basking shark

Hello I'm a basking shark

My mouth is a meter wide

I live in every ocean

I prefer cold waters

To catch food, I swim with my mouth open

I eat small fish, fish eggs and plankton

I migrate in the winter

I can live in a group with up to a hundred sharks

The boys and girls are separate living in two different

groups

I can live to be fifty years old

I'm protected

Beige cat shark

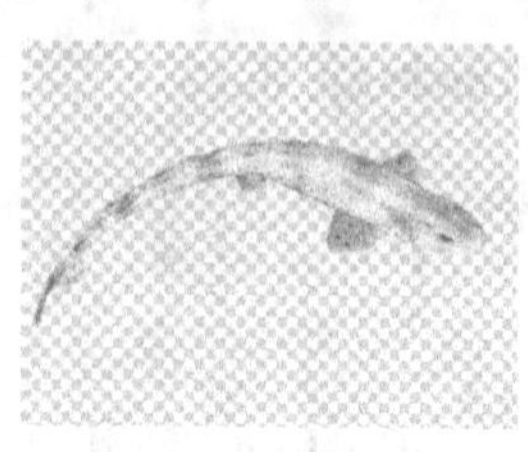

Hello I'm a beige cat shark

I'm awake at night

I live near Australia

I live in the Pacific Ocean

I can be up to seventy-one centimeters long

Big eye sand shark

Hello I'm a big eye sand shark

I like deep warm water

I live in the Atlantic and Pacific Oceans

I can be up to three hundred twenty-six centimeters long

Big eye thresher shark

Hello I'm a big eye thresher

shark

I live all over the world

I like shallow water

I can have up to forty-eight teeth

I'm purple

I can be up to 4.9 meters long

I can live up to twenty years

I eat fish, crab, and bird

I'm hunted for food, vitamins, and leather

# Big head cat shark

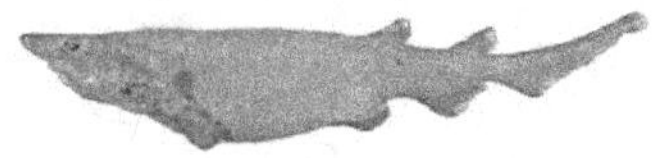

Hello I'm a big head cat shark

I live in the Indian Ocean

I'm awake at night

I like to sleep in a big group during the day

I can be up to 67.5 centimeters long

Bird beak dog fish shark

Hello I'm a bird beak dog fish shark

I live in the Atlantic and Pacific Oceans

I can be up to one hundred twenty-two centimeters long

I eat fish, cephalopods, and crustaceans

Boys and girls live in two separate groups

Black fin gulper shark

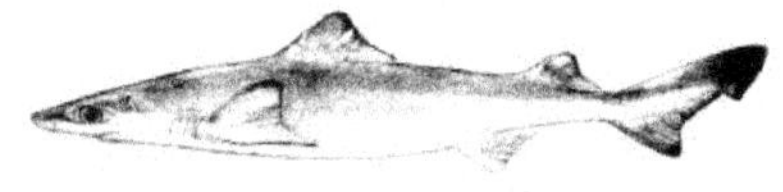

Hello I'm a black fin gulper shark

I like deep water

I'm hunted for oil and fish food

I live in the Indian and Pacific Oceans

Black gill cat shark

Hello I'm a black gill cat shark

I'm awake at night

I like to sleep in a group during the day

I live in the Pacific Ocean

I eat fish, crustaceans, and cephalopods

I can be up to eighty-five centimeters long

Black nose shark

Hello I'm a black nose shark

As a baby I have a black spot on my nose

I am just over four feet long

I eat fish and octopus

people hunt me

I live in the Caribbean Sea

Black rough scale cat shark

Hello I'm a black rough scale cat

shark

I live in the Atlantic and Indian Oceans

I can be up to ninety centimeters long

Black tip reef shark

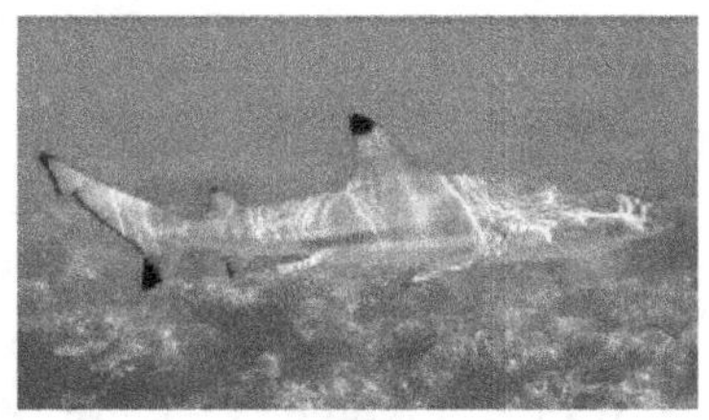

Hello I'm a black tip reef

shark

I eat fish

I can be up to two meters long

I live near south Africa

I live in shallow water

I'm easy to frighten and I try to avoid people

In Hawaii I'm considered a guardian spirit

Black tip shark

Hello I'm a black tip shark

I eat fish, crustaceans, stingrays, and squid

I can be up to eight feet long

I'm almost threatened

I live in warm shallow water

Boys and girls live in two separate groups

I like to leap out of the water

If a mother wants to, she can get herself pregnant without

help

Blind shark

Hello I'm a blind shark

I can have up to sixty-three rows of teeth

I like rocks, coral reefs, and shallow water

I eat invertebrates

I do well in captivity

I live in the Pacific Ocean

I can live up to eighteen hours out of water

I can be up to sixty-six centimeters long

Blotchy swell shark

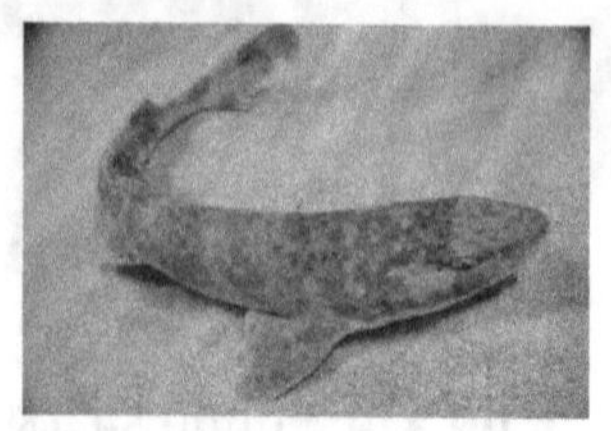

Hello I'm a blotchy swell shark

I eat fish, crustaceans, and cephalopods

I'm awake at night

I sleep in a group during the day

If I'm afraid I inflate my belly with air or water

I like coral reefs

I live in the Pacific Ocean

I can be up to one hundred twenty centimeters long

Blue grey carpet shark

Hello I'm a blue grey carpet

shark

I can be up to seventy-five centimeters long

I live in shallow water near Australia

Blue Shark

Hello I'm a Blue Shark

My teeth are triangular

Boys are bigger than girls

I live all over the world

People see me often

I eat fish, squid, octopus, birds, crabs, lobsters, small
sharks

I'll even eat any dead mammals I find

We hunt in groups sometimes

I'm almost threatened

Blue spotted bamboo shark

Hello I'm a blue spotted bamboo shark

I live in the Indian Ocean

I can be up to sixty-seven centimeters long

Blunt nose six gill shark

Hello I'm a blunt nose six gill

shark

I can be up to sixteen feet long

I'm hunted for food, fish food and oil

I do not like to be touched

I live in the Atlantic and Pacific Oceans

I like deep water

I have green eyes

I can live eighty years

I can be up to 4.8 meters long

I eat fish, dolphins, rays, snails, crab, shrimp, and squid

Bonnet head shark

Hello I'm a bonnet head shark

I can be up to fifty-nine inches long

I'm hunted for food

I live in the Atlantic and Pacific Oceans

I like shallow water and coral reefs

I eat fish, shrimp, crab, mollusk, and seagrass

New parents don't feel hungry

Borneo shark

Hello I'm a Borneo shark

I'm endangered

I live in the Pacific Ocean

I can be up to seventy centimeters long

I have three eyelids on each side of my head

Brachaeluridae

Hello I'm a Brachaeluridae

I live near Australia

I like shallow water

I shut my eyes when I'm out of the water

I eat fish, cuttlefish, crustaceans, and sea anemones

Bramble shark

Hello I'm a bramble shark

I'm hunted for medicine and fish food

I live in the Indian, Pacific, and Atlantic Oceans

I'm slow

I like deep water

I can be up to 3.1 meters long

I eat crab, shark, and fish

Bristly cat shark

Hello I'm a bristly cat shark

I can be up to twenty-six centimeters long

I live in the Indian and Pacific Oceans

I eat fish, squid, and crustaceans

Broad banded lantern shark

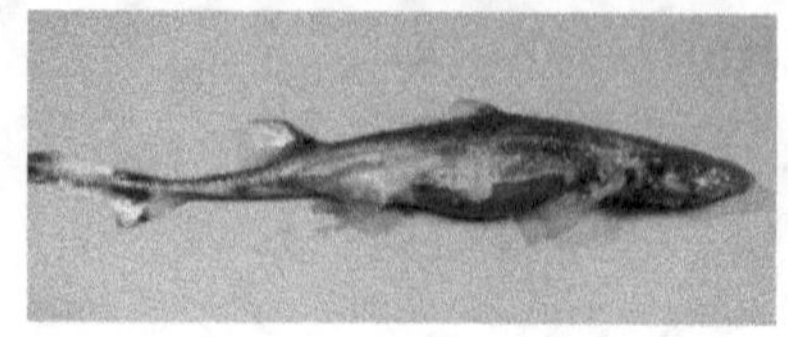

Hello I'm a broad banded lantern shark

I live in the Atlantic Ocean

I like deep water

I can be up to thirty-five centimeters long

I eat fish, squid, octopus, and shrimp

Broad gill cat shark

Hello I'm a broad gill cat shark

I live in the Gulf of Mexico and the Caribbean Sea

I'm awake at night

I sleep in a group during the day

I can be up to forty-six centimeters long

Broad mouth cat shark

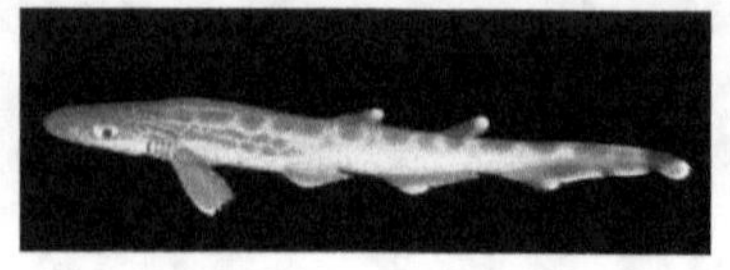

Hello I'm a broad mouth cat shark

I live in the Pacific Ocean

I can be up to thirty-eight centimeters long

I'm awake at night

I sleep in a group during the day

Broad nose cat shark

Hello I'm a broad nose cat

shark

I live in the Indian Ocean

I can be up to twenty-six centimeters long

I'm awake at night

I sleep in a group during the day

Broad nose seven gill shark

Hello I'm a broad nose seven

gill shark

I'm hunted for oil, leather, and food

I live in the Atlantic and Pacific

I like deep water

I'm slow

I can live fifty years

I can be up to three meters long

I eat sharks, rays, fish, and marine mammals

Bronze whaler shark

Hello I'm a bronze whaler shark

I'm also called a copper shark or a narrow tooth shark

I live in the Pacific Ocean

I like warm water

I'm hunted by people

I'm almost threatened

I like to live alone or in a very small group

I eat fish and cephalopods

I herd my prey into a tight ball

Brown shy shark

Hello I'm a brown shy shark

I eat lobsters and fish

Girls can be up to 2.1 feet long

Boys can be up to 2.3 feet long

I live in shallow waters

Full of rocks or sand

If I'm afraid I put my tail over my eyes

# Bull head shark

Hello I'm a bull head shark

I live in the Pacific and Indian Oceans

I like rocks

I eat crustaceans, mollusk, and sea urchins

I like warm shallow water

I put my eggs in cracks in rocks to protect them

I can be up to 5.6 feet long

Bull Shark

Hello I'm a bull shark

Girls are bigger than boys

I live in the Atlantic and Indian oceans

I can live in fresh or salt water

I like to hunt in murky water

I'll eat anything

Even a hippo

When a boy loves a girl, he bites her

I like to live alone

Near people

I'm almost threatened

Bulldog cat shark

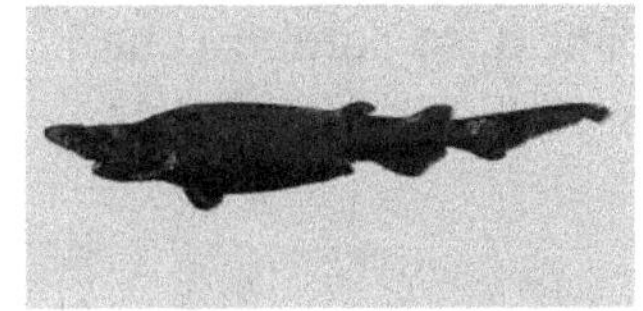

Hello I'm a Bulldog cat shark

I live in the East China Sea

I can be up to fifty-six centimeters long

Burmese bamboo shark

Hello I'm a Burmese bamboo shark

I can be up to 57.5 centimeters long

I like deep water and sand

I live in the Indian Ocean

I like to live alone

I eat fish and invertebrates

I do well in Captivity

Campeche cat shark

Hello I'm a Campeche cat shark

I live in the Gulf of Mexico

I'm awake at night

I sleep in a group during the day

I can be up to sixteen centimeters long

Carcharocles

angustidens

Hello I'm Carcharocles

Angustidens

I lived twenty-two million years ago

I ate penguins, fish, dolphins, and whales

# Caribbean lantern shark

Hello I'm a Caribbean lantern

shark

I live in the Atlantic Ocean

I like sand

I can be up to fifty centimeters long

Caribbean reef Shark

Hello I'm a Caribbean reef

shark

I live in the Atlantic Ocean

I have bigger gills than other sharks

I have two dorsal fins

I can be up to ten meters long

I'm white, yellow, dark grey, or dark brown

People hunt me for food

But that is against the law

I eat fish, rays, crustaceans, and cephalopods

I like to live alone and I try to avoid people

Caribbean rough shark

Hello I'm a Caribbean rough shark

I live in the Gulf of Mexico and the Caribbean Sea

I like deep water

I'm related to the prickly shark

Boys can be up to 1.7 feet long

Carolina hammer head

Hello I'm a Carolina hammer head

I can be up to four meters long

I live in the Atlantic Ocean

I eat sharks, rays, fish, crab, lobster, shrimp, and
cephalopods

I have ten fewer vertebrae then the scalloped hammer
head

Cat shark

Hello I'm a cat shark

I'm all over the world

I live near the bottom of the ocean

I can be up to three feet long

Chain cat shark

Hello I'm a chain cat shark

I'm kept as a pet

I live in the Atlantic Ocean

I like to live among rocks and trash

I eat fish, worms, squid, and crustaceans

I can be up to eighteen inches long

Chilean angel shark

Hello I'm a Chilean angel shark

I'm comfortable at a depth of seventy-five meters

I can be up to one hundred fifty centimeters long

I live in the Pacific Ocean

Cladoselache

Hello I'm Cladoselache

I lived four hundred million years ago

I had a forked tail

I swallowed my food

I did not chew

Cloudy cat shark

Hello I'm a cloudy cat shark

I live in the Pacific Ocean

I like rocks

I have three eyelids on each side of my head

I can be up to fifty centimeters long

I eat mollusk, crustaceans, and fish

The colder my home is the longer I take to mature

Cobbler wobbegong

Hello I'm a cobbler wobbegong

I live near Australia

I like rocks and coral reefs

I can be up to ninety-two centimeters long

I eat crab

Cobelodus

Hello I'm Cobelodus

I lived in the Carboniferous period

I had a round head

I had an arched back

I could be up to two meters long

Comb tooth lantern shark

Hello I'm a comb tooth lantern shark

I live in the South China Sea

I'm comfortable at a depth of six hundred ninety meters

I can be up to twenty-nine centimeters long

Cookie cutter shark

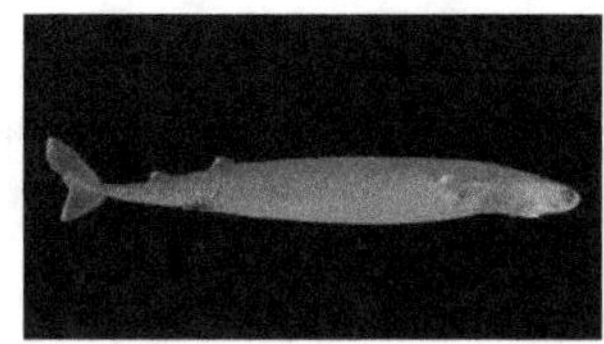

Hello I'm a cookie cutter shark

My belly glows in the dark

I can damage submarines

I live in the Atlantic and Pacific Oceans

I live in deep water

I'm awake at night

I can have up to sixty-eight teeth

Boys can be up to forty-two centimeters long

Girls can be up to fifty-six centimeters long

I eat fish, whales, stingrays, dolphins, seals, and sharks

Coral cat shark

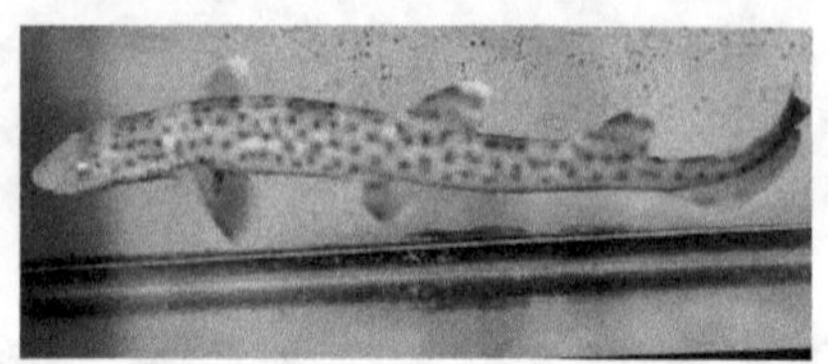

Hello I'm a coral cat shark

I'm awake at night

I live in the Indo-Pacific

I can be up to seventy centimeters long

I eat fish and invertebrates

I'm almost threatened

I do well in captivity

Cosmopolitodus hastalis

Hello I'm Cosmopolitodus

hastalis

I lived three million years ago

My teeth were three inches long

I lived all over the world

My teeth were not serrated

they were triangular

Cow shark

Hello I'm a cow shark

I like cold deep water

I can be up to 15.5 feet long

I live in the Atlantic, Pacific and Indian Oceans

I eat sharks, rays, fish, and seals

Crested bull head shark

Hello I'm a crested bull head shark

I like rocks

I can be up to 1.5 meters long

I live in the Pacific Ocean

I'm awake at night

I eat mollusk, shell fish, fish, and sea urchins

I like to live alone

Cretolamna

Hello I'm Cretolamna

I lived ninety million years ago

I could be up to three meters long

My teeth could be up to two centimeters long

Cretoxyrhina

Hello I'm Cretoxyrhina

I lived eighty-two million years ago

I was seven meters long

I ate fish and turtles

Crocodile shark

Hello I'm a crocodile shark

I live in tropical water

I can be up to one hundred ten centimeters long

I eat eggs

Dagger nose shark

Hello I'm a dagger nose shark

I'm hunted for food

I can live up to twelve years

I can be up to one hundred sixty centimeters long

I live in the Atlantic Ocean

I'm critically endangered

I like shallow warm water

I like mud and mangroves

Dark shy shark


Hello I'm a dark shy shark

I like shallow water

I like sand, kelp, and rocks

I live in the Atlantic Ocean

I eat crustaceans and cephalopods

I can live up to twenty-five years

I can be up to fifty-seven centimeters long

I hide my face with my tail if I'm afraid

Deep water cat shark

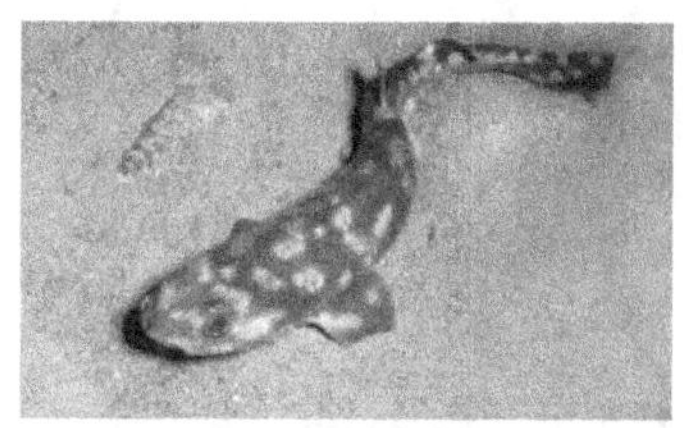

Hello I'm a deep water cat

shark

I live in the Atlantic Ocean

I eat crustaceans, squid, and fish

I like warm water

I can be up to 54.2 centimeters long

Deep water sickle fin hound shark

Hello I'm a deep water sickle fin

hound shark

I live in the Coral Sea

I can be up to sixty centimeters long

Dumb gulper shark

Hello I'm a dumb gulper shark

I'm endangered

I live in the Pacific Ocean

I can be up to one hundred ten centimeters long

I'm hunted for food and fish oil

I can live up to forty-six years

I eat fish, cephalopods, and crustaceans

Dusky shark

Hello I'm a dusky shark

I'm hunted by people for meat and leather

I live in the Mediterranean, the Indian ocean, the Atlantic
Ocean and the Pacific Ocean

I'm vulnerable

Girls and boys live in two separate groups

I can be up to four hundred centimeters long

I eat fish, crustaceans, and cephalopods

Dusky smooth hound

Hello I'm a dusky smooth hound

I live in the Atlantic Ocean

I can be up to one hundred fifty centimeters long

I eat fish, worms, squids, and gastropods

Dwarf lantern shark

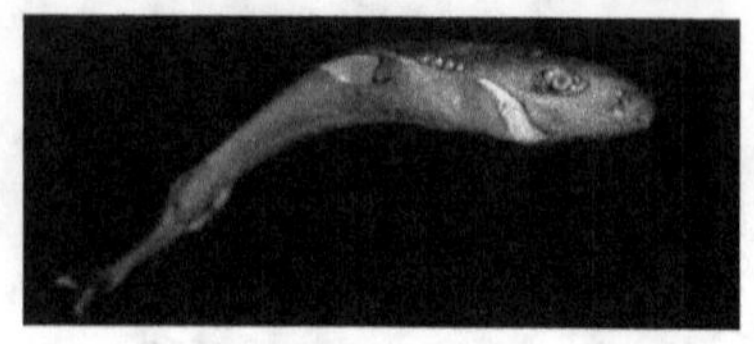

Hello I'm a dwarf lantern shark

I glow in the dark

I'm the smallest shark in the world

I live in the Caribbean Sea

I like shallow water

Dwarf ornate wobbegong

Hello I'm a dwarf ornate

wobbegong

I eat fish

I like shallow warm water and rocks

Boys can be up to eighty-three centimeters long

Girls can be up to eighty-six centimeters long

I bite divers

Dwarf saw tail cat shark

Hello I'm a dwarf saw tail cat shark

I'm awake at night

I live in the Pacific Ocean

I have spines on my tail

I can be up to thirty centimeters long

Dwarf spotted wobbegong

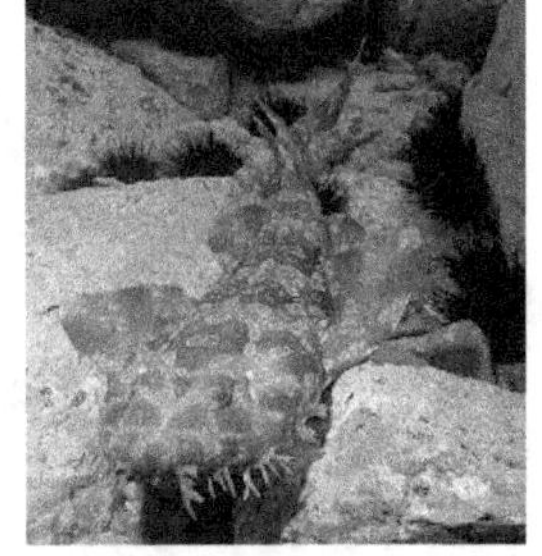

Hello I'm a dwarf spotted

wobbegong

I live in the Indian Ocean

Boys can be up to 88.5 centimeters long

Girls can be up to 94.3 centimeters long

Eastern angel shark

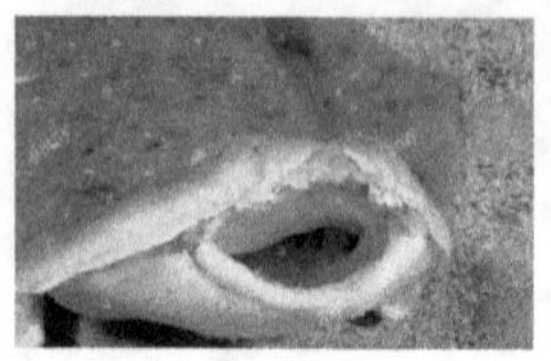

Hello I'm an Eastern angel shark

I live near Australia

I eat crustaceans and cephalopods

I like sand

I'm vulnerable

I can be up to one hundred thirty centimeters long

I live in the Pacific Ocean

Edestus

Hello I'm Edestus

I lived three hundred million years ago

I could be up to twenty feet long

I lived all over the world

# Elegestolepis

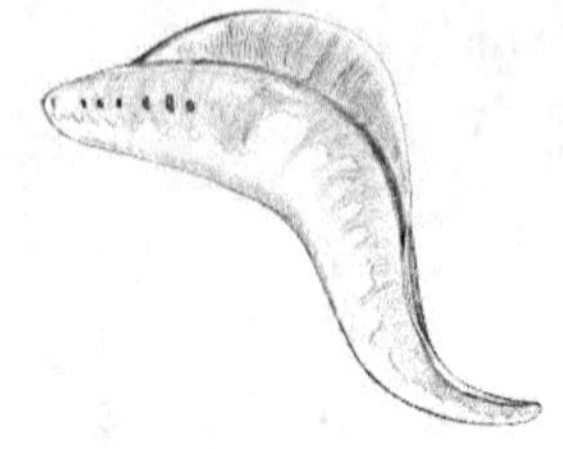

hello I'm Elegestolepis

I lived four hundred and twenty-three million years ago

I lived near Russia

I'm the first shark to have placoid scales

Elephant shark

Hello I'm an elephant shark

I'm a living fossil

My immune system relies on just one type of helper cell

I have evolved slower than any other animal

I'm the link between fish with bones and fish without

bones

Eosqualiolus

Hello I'm an Eosqualiolus

I lived between the Eocene and the Miocene

I lived in France

I only left twenty-eight fossils behind

Epaulette shark

Hello I'm an epaulette shark

I like tidal pools

I can survive out of water for hours

I can crawl on land

I do well in captivity

I live in the Pacific Ocean

I crawl on the sea floor

I like coral reefs

I can be up to sixty-four centimeters long

I eat worms and crustaceans

Falcatus

Hello I'm Falcatus

I lived near America

I could be up to thirty centimeters long

Boys had a spine on their heads to make them look pretty

I liked to hunt in deep water

I lived in the Carboniferous period

False catshark

Hello I'm a false cat shark

I live in deep waters near Scotland

I eat pear, potato and puffer fish

I'm slow

Fedorov's cat shark

Hello I'm Fedorov's cat shark

I live near Japan

I lay eggs

File tail cat shark

Hello I'm a file tail cat shark

I live in the Pacific Ocean

I like deep water

I have very large gills

I can be up to fifty-five centimeters long

I eat fish and invertebrates

Flaccid cat shark

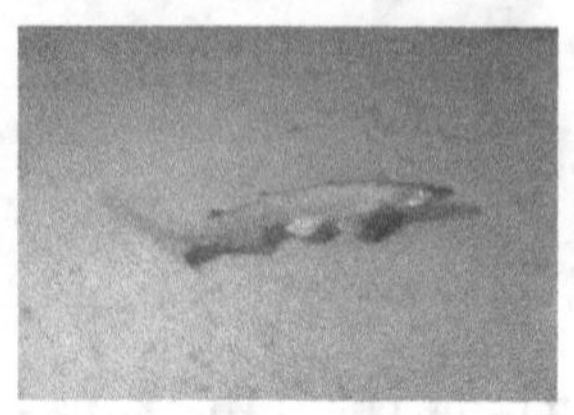

Hello I'm a flaccid cat shark

I live in the Pacific Ocean

I'm comfortable at a depth of 1200 meters

I can be up to 90.8 centimeters long

Flat head cat shark

Hello I'm a flat head cat shark

I live in the Pacific Ocean

I can be up to 67.4 centimeters long

I like deep water

I'm awake at night

I sleep in a group during the day

Floral banded wobbegong

Hello I'm a floral banded

wobbegong

I live in the Indian Ocean

I'm comfortable at a depth of eighty-five meters

I can be up to seventy-five centimeters long

Like all other sharks I'm protected under Australian law

Frilled shark

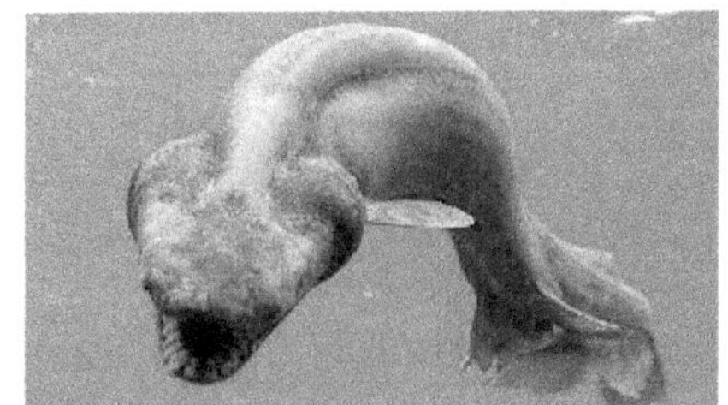

Hello I'm a frilled shark

I live in deep warm water

I can be up to two meters long

I swim like an eel

I eat squid

I'm almost threatened

Fringe fin lantern shark

Hello I'm a fringe fin lantern shark

I'm not threatened

I live in the Atlantic Ocean and the Gulf of Mexico

Frog shark

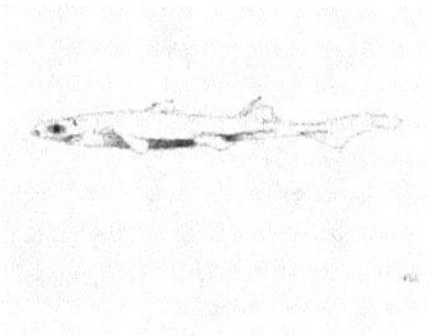

Hello I'm a frog shark

I can be up to one hundred forty-three centimeters long

I'm vulnerable

I live in the Pacific Ocean

I like deep water

Galagadon

Hello I'm a Galagadon

I lived in fresh water

I lived sixty-seven million years ago

I lived in the rivers of South Dakota

I could be up to eighteen inches long

Galapagos bull head shark

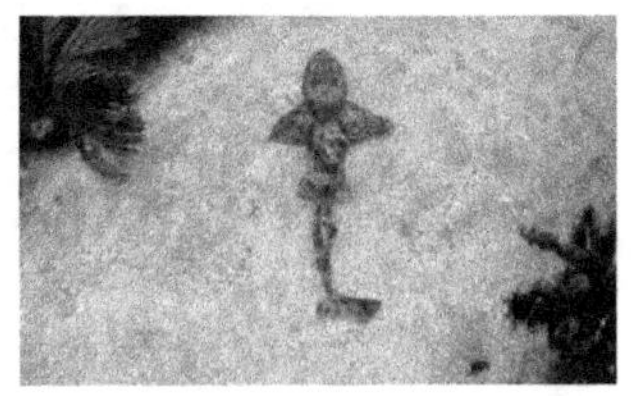

Hello I'm a Galapagos bull head

shark

I eat crab

I like rocks and coral reefs

I can be up to one hundred and seven centimeters long

I live in the Pacific Ocean

I'm awake at night

I like cold water

Galapagos shark

Hello I'm a Galapagos shark

I'm almost threatened

I live in the warm waters of the Pacific and Atlantic

I can be up to 3.7 meters long

I can live up to twenty-four years

I eat sea lions, fish, squid, and octopus

Galeus

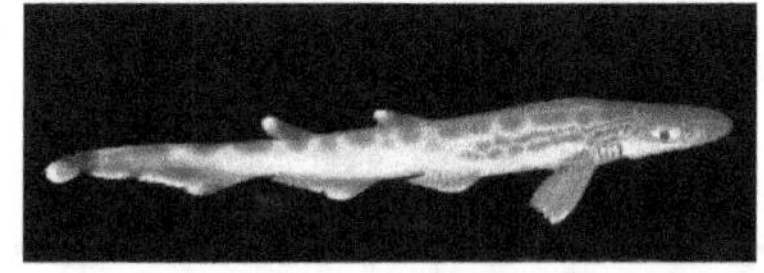

Hello I'm a Galeus

I'm also called the saw tail cat shark

I live in the Atlantic and Pacific Oceans

I like deep water

I eat invertebrates and fish

Ganges shark

Hello I'm a Ganges shark

I live in fresh and salt water

I live in the Indo-Pacific and the Ganges river

I'm hunted for my meat and jaw bone

I can be up to two hundred four centimeters long

I like mud

Ginger carpet shark

Hello I'm a ginger carpet shark

I live in the Indian Ocean

I like deep water

I can be up to seventy-eight centimeters long

Goblin Shark

Hello I'm a Goblin

Shark

I'm a living fossil

I have a long flat nose and between 66 and 115 teeth

 I'm pink

I live in every ocean near the land

I eat fish, crab, and squid

I can move my jaw forward to help me catch food

I'm slow and I'm awake at night

I'm not endangered

I'm not a threat

Great lantern shark

Hello I'm a great lantern shark

I can be up to seventy-five centimeters long

I live in the Atlantic and Pacific Oceans

I like deep water

Great White Shark

Hello I'm a great

white

Girls can be up to six

meters long

Boys can be up to four meters long

 I live all over the world

I eat what I can find

Possibly even a whale

I can live alone or in small groups

If I'm not sure about something I find I bite it to figure

out if it's food

I'm vulnerable

Green lantern shark

Hello I'm a green lantern shark

I live in the Gulf of Mexico, the Atlantic Ocean, and the

Caribbean Sea

I can be up to twenty-six centimeters long

I like the sea floor

Greenland shark

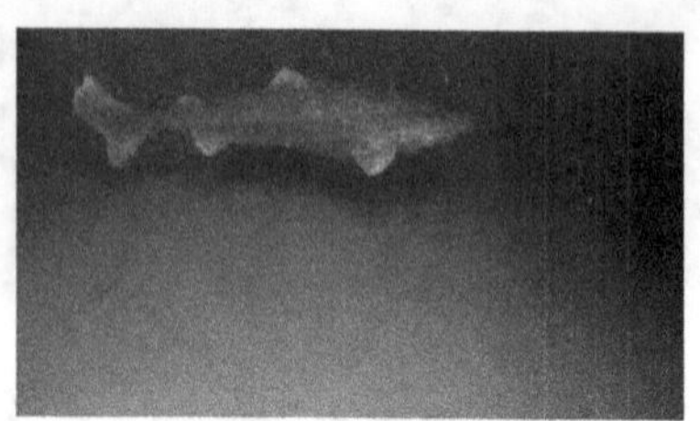

Hello I'm a Greenland shark

I live in cold water

I can be up to seven meters long

I can live over five hundred years

I live in deep water

I eat fish, eels, crustaceans, and horses

I'm slow

My meat is toxic

Grey bamboo shark

Hello I'm a grey bamboo shark

I eat fish, worms, crab, and mollusk

I can be up to seventy-seven centimeters long

I like lagoons, rocks, coral reefs, sand, and mud

I live in the Indian Ocean

I'm almost threatened

I'm slow

Grey reef shark

Hello I'm a Grey reef shark

I live in the Red sea and the Indian ocean

I spent my days in a group and my nights hunting alone

I'm hunted by humans as both pet fish food and meat

I will approach divers

I'm almost threatened

I can be up to seven feet long

I can live for twenty-five years

I eat fish

Gulf wobbegong

Hello I'm a gulf wobbegong

I can be up to 2.9 meters long

I'm closely related to the spotted wobbegong

I live near Australia in the Pacific Ocean

Gulper shark

Hello I'm a gulper shark

I live in the Atlantic, Pacific, and Indian Oceans

I can be up to one hundred ten centimeters long

I'm hunted for oil and food

I'm endangered near Australia

I eat fish, squid, and crustaceans

Gummy shark

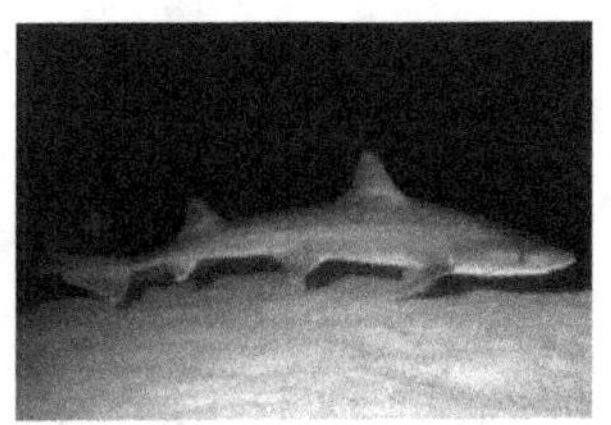

Hello I'm a gummy shark

I'm hunted for food

I can be up to one hundred seventy-five centimeters long

I can live up to sixteen years

I eat crustaceans, cephalopods, worms, and fish

Halmahera epaulette shark

Hello I'm a Halmahera epaulette shark

I use my fins to crawl on the ocean floor

I can be up to sixty-eight centimeters long

I like shallow water

I only live near Halmahera

I eat fish and crustaceans

Hammer head shark

Hello I'm a Hammer head

My head looks like a hammer

I can see three hundred sixty degrees around me

I can be up to six meters long

I live in shallow water

As a baby I have a round head

I live in a group

There can be up to five hundred sharks in one group

I am vulnerable

Hasselt's bamboo shark

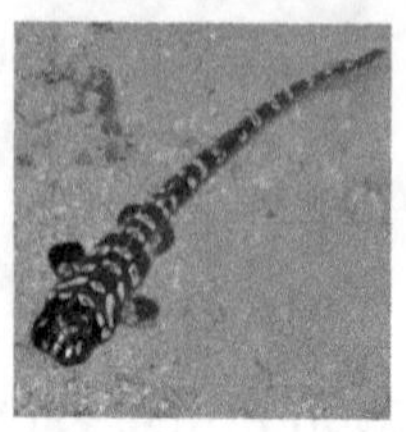

Hello I'm a Hasselt's bamboo shark

I'm almost threatened

I like sand and mud

I like coral reefs

I stick my eggs to plants

I live in the Indian Ocean

I can be up to sixty-one centimeters long

Helicoprion

Hello I'm Helicoprion

I lived two hundred and seventy million years ago

I only had teeth on the bottom of my jaw

I'm the link between sharks and ratfish

I could be up to twenty-five feet long

I ate squid

Hemipristis serra

Hello I'm a Hemipristis serra

I lived 5.3 million years ago

I ate manatee

Hoary cat shark

Hello I'm a hoary cat shark

I am awake at night

I sleep in a group during the day

I live in the Atlantic Ocean

I can be up to 45.5 centimeters long

# Hooded carpet shark

Hello I'm a hooded carpet shark

I live in the Pacific Ocean

I like warm water and coral reefs

I'm awake at night

I'm vulnerable

I can be up to eighty centimeters long

Hook tooth shark

Hello I'm a hook tooth shark

I'm vulnerable

I can be up to one hundred centimeters long

I have three eyelids on each side of my head

I eat fish, crustaceans, and cephalopods

I live in the Indo-Pacific

Horn shark

Hello I'm a horn shark

I can be up to 1.22 Meters long

I like to live alone

I eat crab, fish, mollusk, and sea urchin

I like to live in caves that are sandy or rocky

I live in the Pacific Ocean

I'm awake at night

If a boy shark beats a girl shark in a race, they date

Hump back cat shark

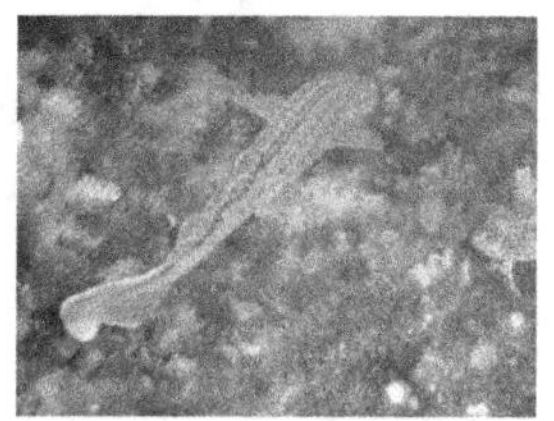

Hello I'm a hump back cat shark

I live in the Pacific Ocean and the South China Sea

I'm awake at night

I sleep in a group during the day

I can be up to 54.2 centimeters long

Hybodus

Hello I'm Hybodus

I lived between the Permian and Cretaceous periods

I looked a lot like modern sharks

I was two meters long

Iago

Hello I'm an Iago

I'm also called a big eye hound shark

I live in the Indian Ocean, Red Sea, and Gulf of Oman

I can be up to fifty-eight centimeters long

Boys and girls live in two separate groups

Girls like shallow water

I eat octopus, squid, and fish

Iceland cat shark

Hello I'm an Iceland cat shark

I live in the Atlantic Ocean

I eat fish, squid, crustaceans, and worms

I like deep water

I can be up to seventy-six centimeters long

I like mud

Indonesian hound shark

Hello I'm an Indonesian hound

shark

I live in the Indian Ocean

I like warm water

I can be up to one hundred twenty centimeters long

Indonesian speckled carpet
shark

Hello I'm an Indonesian speckled carpet shark

I have black speckles on my gills

I'm awake at night

I like shallow water, grass, sand, and coral reefs

I can be up to 66.3 centimeters long

I live in the Pacific Ocean

I'm almost threatened

Indonesian wobbegong

Hello I'm an Indonesian wobbegong

I have twenty-three rows of teeth

I can be up to 3.9 feet long

I like deep cold water

I live in the Pacific Ocean

I'm awake at night

I'm slow

I can live alone or in a group

I like caves

Izak cat shark

Hello I'm an Izak cat shark

I live in the Atlantic and Indian Oceans

I like cool water

I eat fish, eggs, cephalopods, and crustaceans

I like deep water

I can be up to sixty-nine centimeters long

Japanese angel shark

Hello I'm a Japanese angel shark

I have very rough skin

I'm hunted for meat and leather

I have ten rows of teeth

I can be up to one hundred fifty centimeters long

I eat fish, crustaceans, and cephalopods

I live in the Pacific Ocean

Japanese bull head shark

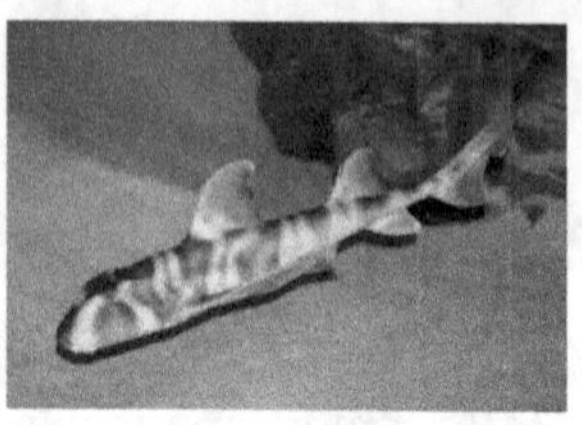

Hello I'm a Japanese bull head

shark

I live in the Pacific Ocean

I like rocks and kelp

I eat invertebrates and fish

I'm slow and docile

I can be up to 1.2 meters long

Girls make nests that many families share

I'm hunted for food

Japanese cat shark

Hello I'm a Japanese cat shark

I live in the Pacific Ocean

I'm awake at night

I sleep in a group during the day

I can be up to seventy-one centimeters long

Japanese saw shark

Hello I'm a Japanese saw shark

I can have up to ninety teeth

I live in the Pacific Ocean

I glow in the dark

My teeth and my scales are made of the same material

My nose is twenty percent of my body length

I like shallow water, mud, and sand

I eat fish, shrimp, and squid

I'm hunted for food

I can be up to 1.5 meters long

Japanese tope shark

Hello I'm a Japanese tope shark

I can be up to 1.1 meters long

I live in the Pacific Ocean

Japanese wobbegong

Hello I'm a Japanese wobbegong

I live in the Pacific Ocean

I'm from the Mesozoic era like all wobbegongs

I like sand, rocks, and coral reefs

I'm slow and I'm a poor swimmer

I can crawl from one tide pool to another

I eat skates and eggs

I'm hunted for food and leather

I do well in captivity

Kite fin shark

Hello I'm a kite fin shark

I can be up to 1.82 meters long

I live in the Atlantic, Pacific and Indian Oceans

I eat fish

I'm hunted for food

I like to live alone

Lake Nicaragua shark

Hello I'm a bull shark

I was once believed to be a different species

I live in fresh water

I can be up to eleven feet long

Lana's saw shark

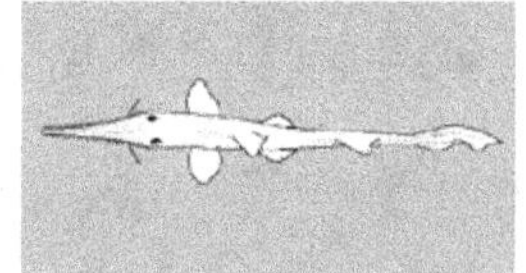

Hello I'm a Lana's saw shark

I live in the Pacific Ocean

Boys can be up to 66.9 centimeters long

Girls can be up to 83 centimeters long

Large tooth cookie cutter shark

Hello I'm a large tooth cookie cutter shark

I like deep water

I live in the Pacific and Atlantic Oceans

I'm a poor swimmer but my liver helps me float

I can be up to forty-two centimeters long

I eat fish and marine mammals

Leaf scale gulper shark

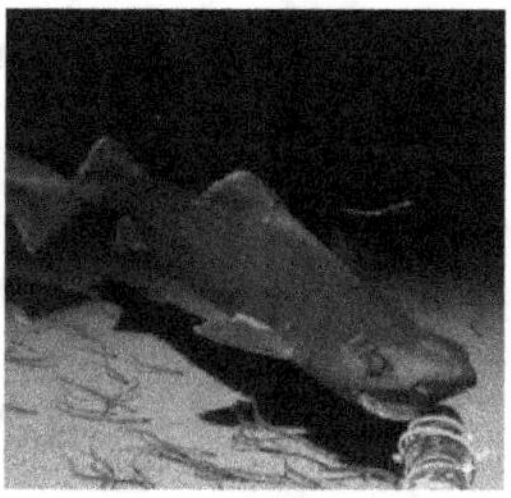

Hello I'm a leaf scale gulper shark

I can be up to one hundred fifty-eight centimeters long

I have green eyes

I live in the Atlantic, Pacific, and Indian Oceans

I eat fish and cephalopods

I'm awake at night

I'm hunted for food and fish food

I like deep water

Lemon Shark

Hello I'm a Lemon Shark

My back is yellow or brown

My mouth is bigger than my nose

I live in the Atlantic Ocean near the shore

It is possible for me to be in rivers

I'm fast

I eat fish, mollusk, crustaceans, birds, and even other
sharks

I live in a group with up to twenty other sharks

I'm almost endangered

People hunt me for food and medicine

Leopard cat shark

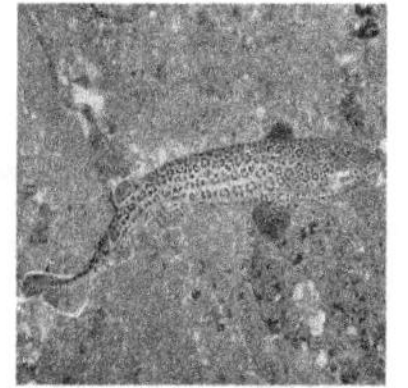

Hello I'm a leopard cat shark

I'm awake at night

I can be up to thirty-three inches long

I live in the Atlantic Ocean

I like warm water and rocks

I eat fish, crustaceans, octopus, and worms

Leopard epaulette shark

Hello I'm a leopard epaulette shark

I like reefs

I live in the Pacific Ocean

I'm awake at night

I can be up to 69.5 centimeters long

Leopard shark

Hello I'm a leopard shark

I can be up to 1.8 meters long

I can weigh up to 18.4 kilograms

I can live up to thirty years

I live in the Pacific Ocean

I eat invertebrates and small sharks

As a new born I'm twenty centimeters long

I'm not endangered

Little gulper shark

Hello I'm a little gulper shark

I eat fish, and squid

I can be up to one hundred ten centimeters long

I'm vulnerable

I live in the Atlantic, Pacific and Indian Oceans

I live in Mediterranean and Arabian seas

I live in the Gulf of Mexico

I'm awake at night

Little sleeper shark

Hello I'm a little sleeper shark

I live in the Atlantic and Pacific Oceans

I live in the Mediterranean Sea

I can be up to 1.43 meters long

I like sand and mud

I eat cephalopods

Long head cat shark

Hello I'm a long head cat shark

I live in the Indo-Pacific

I can have up to eighty-nine rows of teeth

I can be up to sixty centimeters long

I'm both a boy and a girl at the same time

I like deep water

I have three eyelids on each side of my head

Long nose cat shark

Hello I'm a long nose cat shark

I live in the Pacific Ocean

I live at a depth of 1890 meters

I can be up to 58 centimeters long

Long nose saw shark

Hello I'm a long nose saw shark

I can live up to fifteen years

I like to live alone

I eat fish and crustaceans

I can be up to one hundred twenty-five centimeters long

I live in the Indian Ocean

Lost shark

Hello I'm a lost shark

I'm also called a false small tail shark

I have not been seen in eighty years

I like shallow water

I live in the Pacific Ocean and the South China Sea

Low fin gulper shark

Hello I'm a low fin gulper shark

I'm vulnerable

I like deep water

I can be up to 3.3 feet long

I live in the Atlantic and Indian Oceans

I live in the Mediterranean Sea

I eat sharks, fish, and cephalopods

I'm hunted for food

Mako Shark

Hello I'm a Mako Shark

I'm fast and I like to jump

I'm dangerous

I'm grey or blue

The girls are bigger than the boys

I live all over the world

I prefer warm waters

I eat fish, squid, octopus, birds, turtles and smaller sharks

No other shark is faster than me

I prefer to live alone but might live in a group

I'm considered vulnerable

Marbled cat shark

Hello I'm a marbled cat shark

I'm also called an Australian marbled cat shark

I like sand and rocks

I do well in captivity

I live in the Indian Ocean

McMillan's cat shark

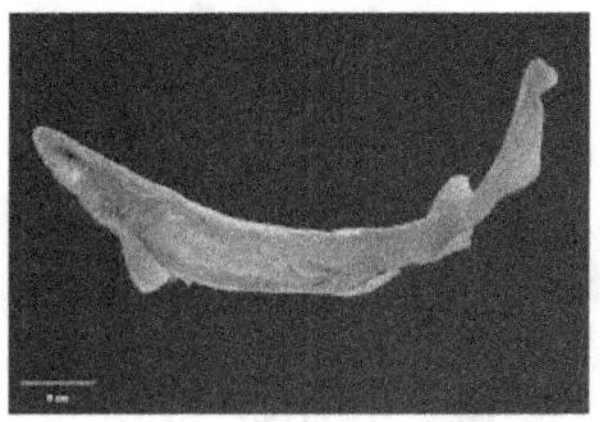

Hello I'm a McMillan's cat shark

I live in the Indian and Pacific Oceans

I can be up to forty-five centimeters long

I'm awake at night

I sleep in a group during the day

I eat cephalopods, crustaceans, and fish

I like deep water

Megalodon

Hello I'm Megalodon

I lived twenty million years ago

I had two hundred seventy-six teeth

I was more than twenty meters long

I ate two thousand five hundred kilograms of food every

day

Megamouth Shark

Hello I'm a megamouth Shark

I'm black or brown

I'm small and slow

I glow to attract my prey

I live in deep waters

I eat plankton, jellyfish, and shrimp

I'm not easy to observe

I'm not endangered

Mexican horn shark

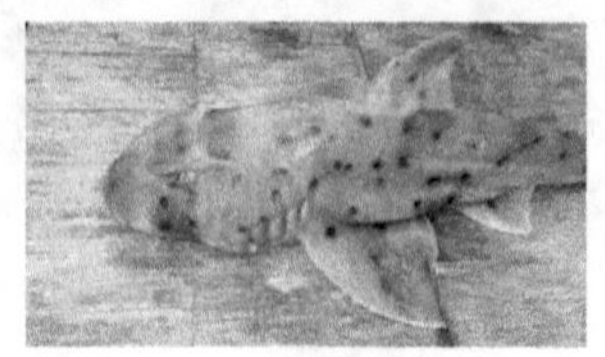

Hello I'm a Mexican horn shark

I eat crabs and fish

I can be up to seventy centimeters long

I like coral reefs, sand and rocks

I live in the Pacific Ocean

Mongolepis

Hello I'm Mongolepis

I lived four hundred and twenty million years ago

I lived near Mongolia

No one is sure how big I was

Or what I ate

Mosaic gulper shark

Hello I'm a mosaic gulper shark

I like deep water

I live in the Pacific Ocean

I can be up to eighty-nine centimeters long

Mouse cat shark

Hello I'm a mouse cat shark

I have three eyelids on each side of my head

I can be up to sixty-three centimeters long

I live in the Atlantic Ocean

I like deep water

I eat shrimp, fish, and cephalopods

Narrow mouthed cat shark

Hello I'm a narrow mouthed cat shark

I eat fish, crustaceans, and cephalopods

I live in the Atlantic and Pacific Oceans

I'm awake at night

I sleep in a group during the day

I can be up to seventy centimeters long

Narrow tail cat shark

Hello I'm a narrow tail cat shark

I like deep water

I can be up to thirty-three centimeters long

I eat fish and cephalopods

I live in the Atlantic Ocean

I have white spots

Natal shy shark

Hello I'm a natal shy shark

I live in the Indian Ocean

I like shallow water

I do not travel far

I'm critically endangered

Necklace carpet shark

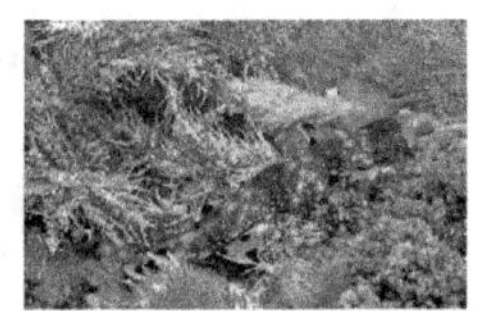

Hello I'm a necklace carpet shark

I like sand, rocks, kelp, and seagrass

I live in the Pacific Ocean

I'm awake at night

I can be up to ninety-one centimeters long

I eat invertebrates

Negaprion eurybathrodon

Hello I'm a Negaprion eurybathrodon

I'm a kind of lemon shark

I lived during the Pliocene

# Northern river shark

Hello I'm a northern river shark

I can live in fresh or salt water

I live around Australia and New Guinea

I'm critically endangered

I eat fish

I like mud

I can be up to one hundred forty-five centimeters long

Northern wobbegong

Hello I'm a northern wobbegong

I like warm shallow water

I like rocks, caves, mud, and coral reefs

I eat invertebrates and fish

I can be up to sixty-three centimeters long

I'm awake at night

I live in the Indian and Pacific Oceans

Nurse shark

Hello I'm a nurse shark

I used to be hunted for oil and leather

I live in the Atlantic Ocean

I like caves, sand, rocks, and shallow water

I can be up to three hundred eight centimeters

I eat coral, algae, mollusk, crustaceans, fish, and stingray

I'm awake at night

Oceanic white tip Shark

Hello I'm an Oceanic white tip

shark

I have a lot of other names

I'm very dangerous

I'm hunted for meat and leather

I live in the Indian, Atlantic, and Pacific Oceans

I do not like shallow waters

I like to live alone

Remoras and similar fish follow me around

I can be up to three meters long

I eat fish, squid, crustaceans, turtles, birds, stingrays, and

gastropods

Ocellated angel shark

Hello I'm an ocellated

angel shark

I live in the Pacific Ocean

I can be up to 2.1 feet long

I like mud

I spend most of my day laying in one spot

I'm vulnerable

I bite whatever touches me

I breath differently from other sharks as my gills both pull

in and pump out water

Oman bull head shark

Hello I'm an Oman bull head shark

I live in the Indian Ocean

Boys can be up to fifty-six centimeters long

Girls can be up to sixty-one centimeters long

My eggs have tendrils

Orectolobus hutchinsi

Hello I'm an Orectolobus hutchinsi

I'm also called a western wobbegong

I like rocks

I live between Bremer Bay and Coral Bay

I can be up to 1.5 meters long

Orectolobus reticulatus

Hello I'm an Orectolobus reticulatus

I'm also called a network wobbegong

I live near Kimberley

I like shallow water

I can be up to 52.3 centimeters long

Ornate wobbegong

Hello I'm an Ornate wobbegong

I live in the Pacific Ocean

I like shallow water and coral reefs

I'm awake at night

I can be up to one hundred twenty centimeters long

I'm almost threatened

Orthacanthus

Hello I'm Orthacanthus

I could be up to three meters long

I ate meat

I lived in fresh water swamps

I lived from the Devonian to the Triassic period

Otodus

Hello I'm Otodus

I lived all over the world

I lived sixty million years ago

I could be up to thirty feet long

I ate whales

Pacific angel shark

Hello I'm a Pacific angel shark

I live in the Pacific Ocean

I have nineteen rows of teeth

I can be up to one hundred fifty-two centimeters long

I like kelp, shallow water, and rocks

I eat fish and squid

I like to bury myself in sand

Pacific sleeper shark

Hello I'm a pacific sleeper shark

I like deep water

I can be up to seven meters long

My meat is toxic

I live in the Pacific Ocean

Pale cat shark

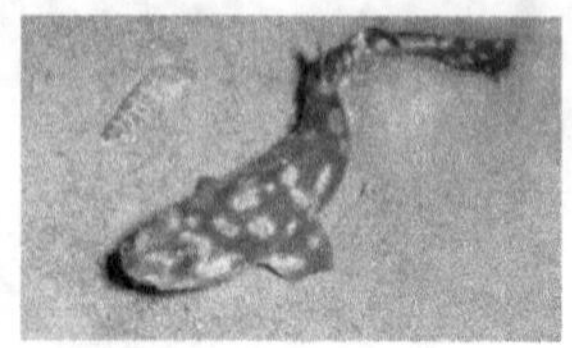

Hello I'm a Pale cat shark

I live in the Pacific Ocean

I'm awake at night

I sleep in a group during the day

I can be up to twenty-one centimeters long

Panama ghost cat shark

Hello I'm a Panama ghost cat

shark

I'm only in Panama

I'm awake at night

I sleep in a group during the day

I can be up to twenty-three centimeters long

Papuan epaulette shark

Hello I'm a Papuan epaulette shark

I like seagrass, coral reefs, and rocks

I can be up to seventy-seven centimeters long

I like shallow water

I eat shrimp, crab, fish, and sea urchins

I live in the Pacific Ocean

Parascyllildea

Hello I'm a Parascyllildea

No one really knows anything about me

As a shark I have a cartilage skeleton so I did not make

good fossils

Pelagic thresher shark

Hello I'm a pelagic thresher shark

I'm hunted for food and oil

I try to avoid people

I live in the Pacific and Indian Oceans

I can be up to 16.4 feet long

I can live up to 28 years

I eat fish and sometimes squid

My tail cuts my food like a knife

Pencil shark

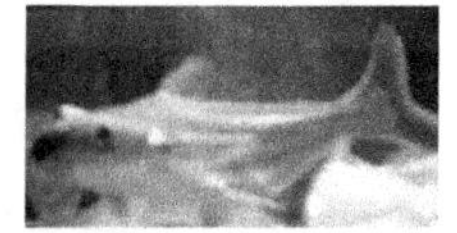

Hello I'm a pencil shark

I live around Australia

I like deep water

I can be up to 1.27 meters long

Pinocchio cat shark

Hello I'm a Pinocchio cat shark

I like deep water and sea mounds

I can be up to eighty-three centimeters long

I live in the Indian and Pacific Oceans

Plunket shark

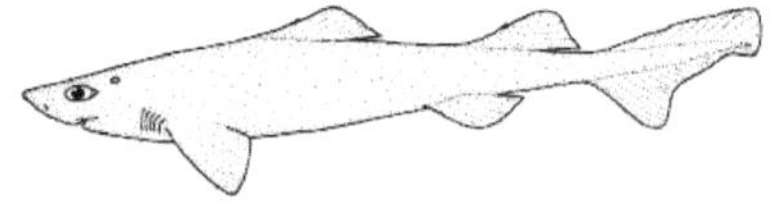

Hello I'm a Plunket shark

I live in the Pacific Ocean

Girls like deep water

Boys and girls live in two separate large groups

I can be up to one hundred seventy centimeters long

I'm hunted for oil and fish food

I eat cephalopods and fish

Pocket shark

Hello I'm a pocket shark

I live in the Pacific Ocean and the Gulf of Mexico

On average I'm fourteen centimeters long

I have pockets on my face

I glow in the dark

Polymerolepis

hello I'm Polymerolepis

I lived four hundred and twenty million years ago

I lived near Mongolia

I was one of the first sharks

Pondicherry shark

Hello I'm a Pondicherry shark

I can live in fresh or salt water

I live in the Indo-Pacific and the Hooghli and Saigon

rivers

I'm critically endangered

I have not been seen in thirty-nine years

I can be up to one meter long

Porbeagle shark

Hello I'm a porbeagle shark

I'm vulnerable

I'm endothermic

I live in the Atlantic and Pacific Oceans

I can be up to two meters long

I can live up to forty-six years in the Atlantic and

sixty-five years in the Pacific

I'm hunted for sport and food

Port Jackson shark

Hello I'm a Port Jackson shark

I can be up to 5.5 feet long

I'm slow

I live near Australia

I like caves

I like to be near shore

Boys and girls live in two different groups

I can live more than thirty years

I eat mollusk, fish, sea urchins, crustaceans, and echinoderms

Prickly shark

Hello I'm a prickly shark

I live in the Pacific Ocean

I eat fish, sharks, rays, and cephalopods

I can be up to four meters long

Pristiophorus striatus

Hello I'm a Pristiophorus striatus

I lived during the Miocene

I lived in Slovakia

I liked deep water

Ptychodus

Hello I'm a Ptychodus

I could be up to ten meters long

I lived in the cretaceous period

I ate shellfish and crustaceans

I lived near the bottom of the ocean

Puff adder shy shark

Hello I'm a puff adder shy shark

I'm almost threatened

I live in the Atlantic Ocean

I like sand and rocks

As a baby I like deep cold water

I can be up to 23.6 inches long

I eat fish, crab, shrimp, and squid

Pygmy ribbon tail cat shark

Hello I'm a pygmy ribbon tail cat shark

I live in the Pacific and Indian Oceans

I like mud

I can be up to twenty-four centimeters long

I eat fish, crustaceans, and squid

Pygmy shark

Hello I'm a pygmy shark

I can be up to twenty-seven centimeters long

I live in the Atlantic, Pacific, and Indian Oceans

I eat squid, crustaceans, and fish

Pyjama shark

Hello I'm a Pyjama shark

I'm also called a lined cat shark or a striped cat shark

I can be up to ninety-five centimeters long

I live in rocky areas and caves

I live in the Atlantic and Indian Oceans

I eat fish, hag fish, small sharks, and eggs

I'm awake at night

I do well in captivity

Quagga cat shark

Hello I'm a quagga cat shark

I live in the Indian Ocean

I like deep water

I can be up to thirty-seven centimeters long

Girls have two sets of private places

Red spotted cat shark

Hello I'm a red spotted cat shark

I'm also called a Chilean cat shark

I like rocks

In the summer I live in shallow water

In the winter I live in deep water

I like to live alone in a cave

I eat crustaceans and invertebrates

I live in the Pacific Ocean

I can be up to sixty-two centimeters long

Requiem shark

Hello I'm a requiem shark

I can be up to twenty-four feet long

I eat birds, mammals, fish, lobster, sharks, rays, squid,

octopus, and turtle

I'm fast

Reticulated swell shark

Hello I'm a reticulated swell shark

I'm awake at night

I sleep in a group during the day

I eat fish, crustaceans, and cephalopods

I can be up to forty-two centimeters long

I like coral reefs

I live in the Pacific Ocean

River shark

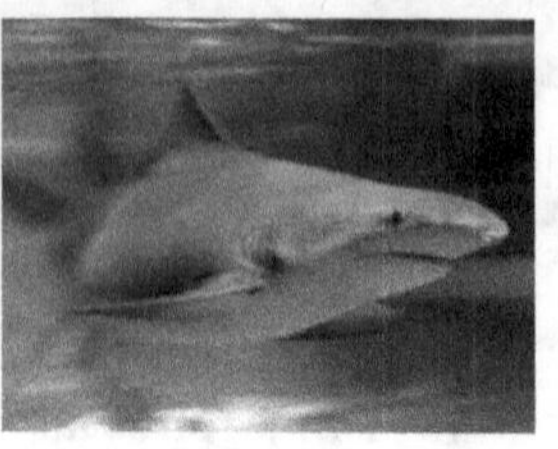

Hello I'm a river shark

I'm also called a glyphis

I live in the Indo-Pacific

I live in fresh and salt water

Rough skin cat shark

Hello I'm a rough skin cat shark

I live in the Pacific Ocean

I like deep water

I can be up to 85.5 centimeters long

Rusty carpet shark

Hello I'm a rusty carpet shark

I like rivers and rocks

I'm awake at night

I live in the Indian Ocean

I eat crustaceans and mollusk

I can be up to eighty centimeters long

Saddle carpet shark

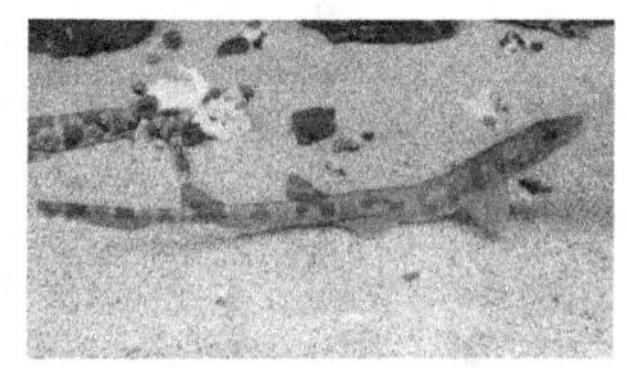

Hello I'm a saddle carpet shark

I have nine spots

I can be up to 48.5 centimeters long

I live in the Pacific Ocean

I live near Japan

Salamander shark

Hello I'm a salamander shark

I'm also called a salamander cat shark

I'm awake at night

I sleep in a group during the day

I like deep water

I live in the Pacific Ocean

I can be up to sixty-four centimeters long

Saldanha cat shark

Hello I'm a Saldanha cat shark

I can be up to 88.5 centimeters long

I eat fish and cephalopods

I live in the Atlantic Ocean

Salmon shark

Hello I'm a salmon shark

I'm endothermic

I can be up to ten feet long

I eat salmon

I live in the Pacific Ocean

I like cool water

I can live up to twenty-seven years

Sand devil

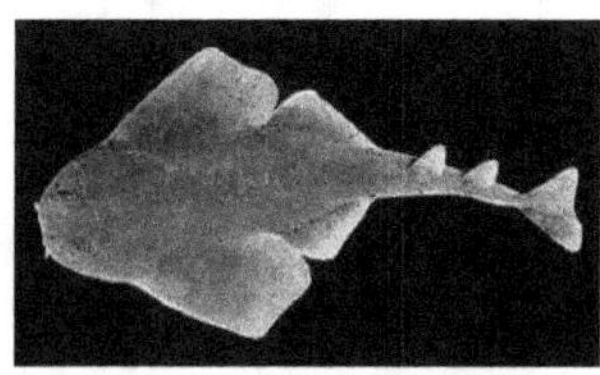

Hello I'm a sand devil

I'm also called an Atlantic angel shark

I live in the Atlantic Ocean

I spend winter in deep water

I spend the rest of the year in shallow water

I can be up to one hundred fifty-two centimeters long

I eat fish and crustaceans

I like sand and mud

I bite diver who touch me

Sand tiger shark

Hello I'm a sand tiger

shark

I'm also called a grey nurse shark

I can live fifteen years

I can be up to 10.5 feet long

I'm vulnerable

I live in warm shallow waters

I eat fish, squid, and crustaceans

I like to fill my belly with air and float near the ocean

floor

Sandbar shark

Hello I'm a sandbar shark

I'm hunted for food

I live in the Atlantic and Pacific Oceans

As well as the Persian Gulf and Red Sea

Girls live alone

Boys live in a group

I like shallow water

I eat fish, eel, rays, octopus, crab, squid, and shrimp

Saw back angel shark

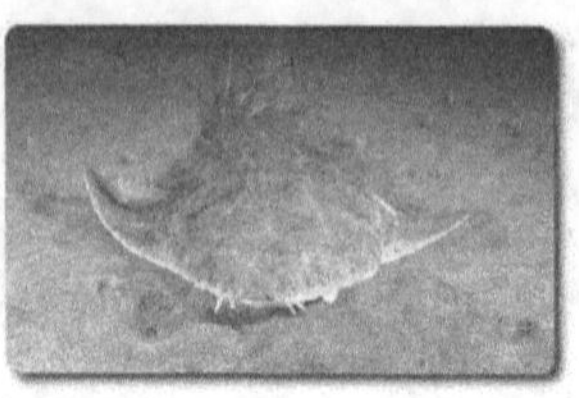

Hello I'm a saw back angel shark

I'm endangered

I live in the Atlantic Ocean and Mediterranean Sea

I can be up to two meters long

I like mud

I eat fish and crustaceans

I'm protected by Spanish law

Saw shark

Hello I'm a saw shark

I can find prey buried in the sand

I live in tropical waters

I can be up to five feet long

Scalloped bonnet head

shark

Hello I'm a scalloped bonnet head shark

I live in the Pacific Ocean

I can be up to ninety-two centimeters long

I like estuaries and mangroves

I eat mollusk and crustaceans

I'm almost threatened

Scalloped hammer head shark

Hello I'm a scalloped hammer

head shark

I'm endangered

I live in warm water

I try to avoid people

I live in a large group or alone depending on the time of

year

I eat stingray

I can be up to four meters long

Scaparnohinchus

Hello I'm Scaparnohinchus

My cousin is the goblin shark

I could be up to sixty-five centimeters long

School shark

Hello I'm a school shark

I can be up to one hundred seventy-five centimeters long

I live in the Indian, Pacific, and Atlantic Oceans

I live in the Mediterranean and Black Seas

I travel far and wide

I eat fish and cephalopods

I can live up to sixty years

As a baby I have black spots on my fins

I live in a big group

Scoop head shark

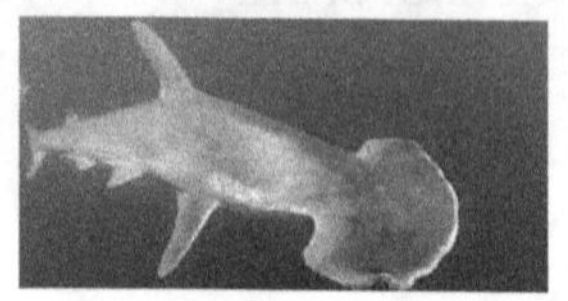

Hello I'm a scoop head shark

I like warm water

I live in the Atlantic and Pacific Oceans

I can be up to one hundred fifty centimeters long

Sharp nose seven gill
shark

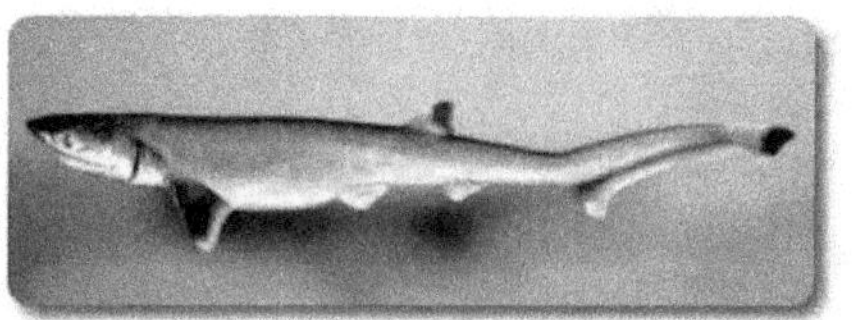

Hello I'm a sharp nose seven gill shark

My meat makes people sick

I live in warm deep water

In the Atlantic and Pacific Oceans

I can be up to 4.5 feet long

I eat invertebrates and fish

I'm awake at night

Sharp tooth hound shark

Hello I'm a sharp tooth hound

shark

I like rocks, gullies, and sand

I can be up to one hundred seventy centimeters long

I eat crustaceans, cephalopods, and fish

I might follow my prey on shore

I live in the Atlantic Ocean

In the summer I live in a group

I like shallow water

I can live up to twenty-five years

I'm almost threatened

Sharp tooth lemon shark

Hello I'm a sharp tooth lemon

shark

I live in the Indian and Pacific Oceans

I like coral reefs, lagoons, and swamps

I'm hunted for food

I'm vulnerable

I can be at least three hundred ten centimeters

I eat fish, sharks, and stingrays

Short fin mako shark

Hello I'm a short fin mako shark

I'm endothermic

I can be up to four meters long

I'm hunted for food

I eat sharks, fish, turtles, squids, porpoises, and dolphins

I can swim up to thirty-five kilometers per hour

I like warm water

I like to jump

I can jump up to six meters out of the water

Short nose demon cat shark

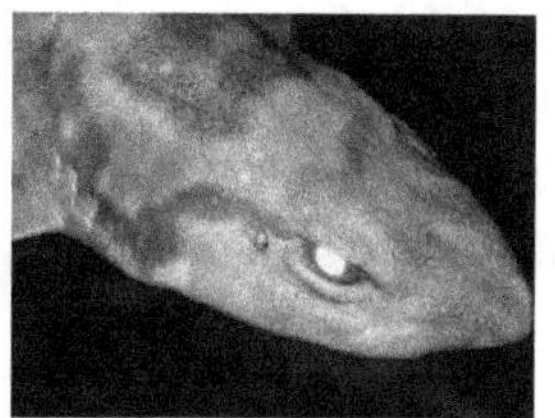

Hello I'm a short nose demon cat shark

I'm awake at night

I sleep in a group during the day

I live in the Pacific Ocean

I like deep water

I can be up to 49.1 centimeters long

Short nose saw shark

Hello I'm a short nose saw shark

I eat invertebrates and fish

I live in the Indian Ocean

I can be up to one hundred twenty-four centimeters long

Short tail lantern shark

Hello I'm a short tail lantern shark

I can be up to fifty centimeters long

I like deep water

I live in the Pacific Ocean

Short tail nurse shark

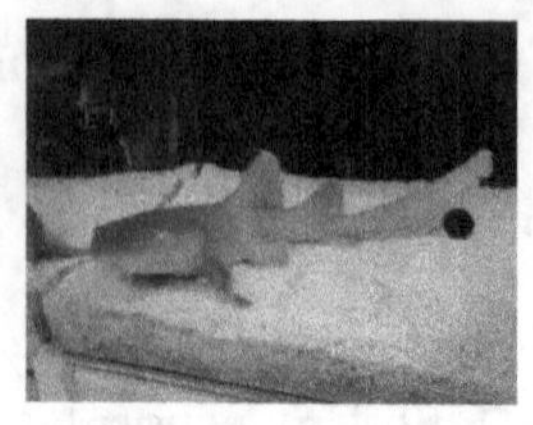

Hello I'm a short tail nurse shark

I like coral reefs and shallow warm water

I can be up to thirty years old

I can be up to seventy-five centimeters long

I can live for many hours out of water

I live in the Indian Ocean

Sickle fin hound shark

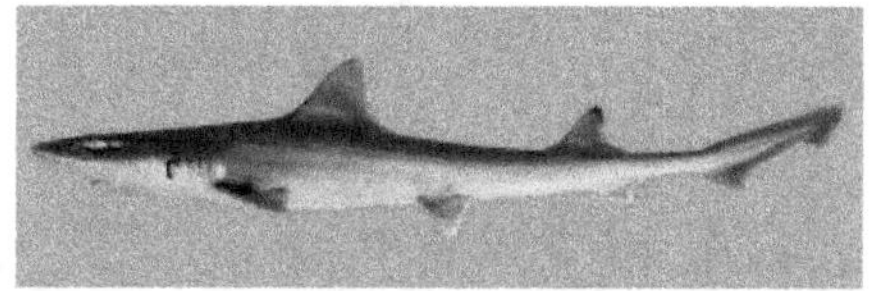

Hello I'm a sickle fin hound shark

I like shallow water

I can live up to twenty-two years

I can be up to one hundred seventy-five centimeters long

I live in the Pacific Ocean

Sickle fin lemon shark

Hello I'm a sickle fin lemon shark

I can be up to fourteen feet long

I'm shy

I'm hunted for oil and food

I'm vulnerable

I live in the Red sea and Indo-Pacific

I like shallow sandy water and coral reefs

I eat sharks, stingray, and fish

Sickle fin weasel shark

Hello I'm a sickle fin weasel shark

I live in the Indian and Pacific Oceans

I like shallow water

I eat cephalopods, crustaceans, and echinoderms

I can be up to one hundred fourteen centimeters long

I'm vulnerable

Silky shark

Hello I'm a silky shark

I'm hunted by people for many reasons

I'm vulnerable

I live in the Caribbean and Red seas as well as the Gulf of

Mexico and the Atlantic, Pacific, and Indian Oceans

I live in a small group

We follow tuna around

Silver tip shark

Hello I'm a silver tip shark

I can weigh up to three hundred pounds

I can be up to ten feet long

I live in the Red Sea and the Pacific and Indian Oceans

People hunt me for meat

I like to live near reefs

I eat fish, squid, shark, and octopus

Six gill saw shark

Hello I'm a six gill saw shark

I like warm water

I eat fish, crustaceans, and squid

Like all sharks I can sense the electricity in my prey's

nervous system

I can be up to one hundred thirty-six centimeters long

I'm almost threatened

I live in the Indian Ocean

Slender bamboo shark

Hello I'm a slender bamboo

shark

I live in the Pacific and Indian Oceans

I can be up to sixty-five centimeters long

I'm hunted for food

I'm slow

I like mud, sand, rocks, and coral reefs

I eat fish and invertebrates

Slender weasel shark

Hello I'm a slander weasel shark

I have three eyelids on each side of my head

I can be up to 48.3 centimeters long

I'm hunted for food

I'm almost threatened

I live in the Indian Ocean

Slit eye shark

Hello I'm a slit eye shark

I live in the Indian Ocean

I can be up to ninety-eight centimeters long

I eat fish, crustaceans, and cephalopods

Small belly cat shark

Hello I'm a small belly cat shark

I live in the Indian Ocean

I like deep water

I live in the Arabian Sea

I can be up to thirty-four centimeters long

Small dorsal cat shark

Hello I'm a small dorsal cat shark

I'm awake at night

I sleep in a group during the day

I can be up to 37.2 centimeters long

I live in the Pacific Ocean

Small eye cat shark

Hello I'm a Small eye cat shark

I live in the Atlantic Ocean

I can be up to sixty-one centimeters long

Small eye hammer head

Hello I'm a small eye hammer head

I'm hunted for food

I'm vulnerable

I live in warm muddy shallow water

I might live in a group

I can be up to one hundred forty-eight centimeters long

I eat shrimp, crabs, sharks, squid, and catfish

Small eye pygmy shark

Hello I'm a small eye pygmy shark

I live between Japan and Australia

I can have up to fifty rows of teeth

I can be up to twenty-two centimeters long

I eat squid, krill, fish, and shrimp

Small fin cat shark

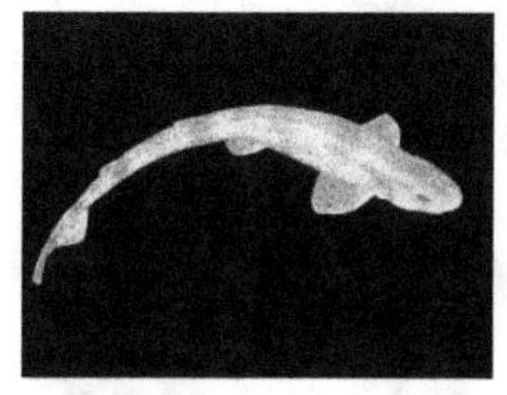

Hello I'm a small fin cat shark

I'm awake at night

I sleep in a group during the day

I live in the Caribbean Sea and Atlantic Ocean

I can be up to fifty-two centimeters long

Small fin gulper shark

Hello I'm a small fin gulper shark

I live in the Pacific and Indian Oceans

I can be up to one hundred centimeters long

I like deep water

I eat fish and crustaceans

Small tooth sand shark

Hello I'm a small tooth sand shark

I can be up to 4.1 meters long

I like rocks and deep warm water but I will enter shallow water

I eat fish and invertebrates

I live in the Atlantic, Pacific, and Indian Oceans

I like coral reefs but also open water

I live in the Mediterranean Sea

I like sand

I'm hunted for food, oil, and my jaw

I'm protected by Australian law

Smooth hammer head shark

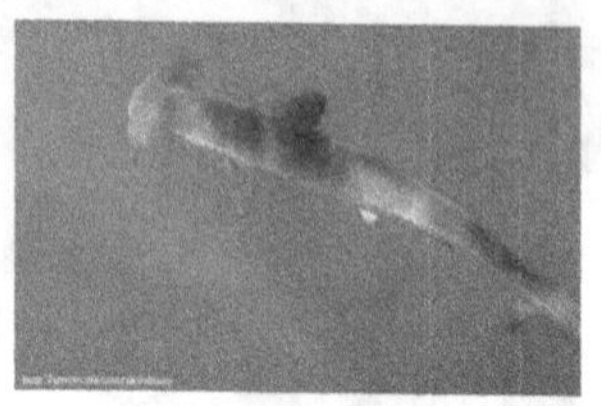

Hello I'm a smooth hammer head

shark

I'm vulnerable

I live in warm waters

I can be up to five meters long

I like shallow water

I eat fish, rays, sharks, dolphins, crustaceans, and

cephalopods

Smooth hound

Hello I'm a smooth hound

Girls can be up to 164 centimeters long

Boys can be up to 110 centimeters long

I live in the Atlantic and Indian Oceans

Near the bottom

I eat crustaceans, Cephalopods, and fish

I'm used as food, fish food, and a source of oil

I'm also kept as a pet

Snaggle tooth shark

Hello I'm a snaggle tooth shark

I lived during the Eocene

I lived in the eastern hemisphere

I could be up to eight feet long

I ate fish, crustaceans, and sharks

South China cat shark

Hello I'm a south China cat shark

I live in the South China Sea

I live in the Pacific Ocean

I'm awake at night

I sleep in a group during the day

I can be up to eighty-two centimeters long

South China cookie cutter shark

Hello I'm a south China cookie

cutter shark

I can be up to 1.4 feet long

I have 43 rows of teeth

I live in the Pacific Ocean and South China Sea

Southern African frilled shark

Hello I'm a southern African

frilled shark

I live near southern Angola

I like deep water

I can be up to one hundred seventeen centimeters long

Southern sleeper shark

Hello I'm a southern sleeper shark

I live in the Atlantic, Pacific, and Indian Oceans

I like deep water

I can be up to 4.4 meters long

I'm slow

I eat birds, marine mammals, fish, and cephalopods

Spatula nose cat shark

Hello I'm a spatula nose cat

shark

I'm also called a Borneo cat shark

I live in the Pacific and Indian Oceans

I can be up to seventy-one centimeters long

Spear tooth shark

Hello I'm a spear tooth shark

I live in the Pacific Ocean

I can live in fresh and salt water

I like mud

I eat fish

I can be up to one hundred seventy-five centimeters long

I'm endangered

Speckled carpet shark

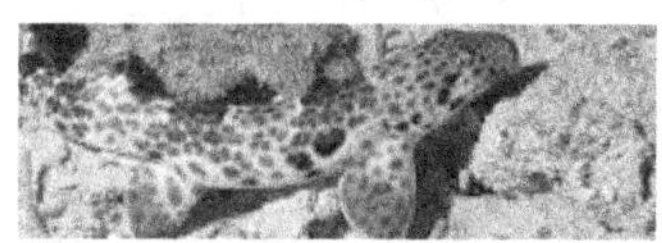

Hello I'm a speckled carpet shark

I like warm shallow water and coral reefs

I can be up to seventy-nine centimeters long

I eat invertebrates

I live in the Pacific Ocean

I'm protected by Australian law because I live in

the Great Barrier Reef Marine Park

Spined pygmy shark

Hello I'm a spined pygmy shark

I can have up to fifty-two rows of teeth

I can be up to twenty-two centimeters long

I eat fish and squid

I glow in the dark

I like deep water

I live in the Indian, Pacific, and Atlantic Oceans

Spinner shark

Hello I'm a spinner shark

I spin as I jump out of the water

I'm hunted by people for meat and leather

I'm almost threatened

I live in the Red Sea and Atlantic Ocean

I live in a group

I need very salty water

I can have up to thirty-one teeth

Spiny dog fish shark

Hello I'm a spiny dog fish

shark

I live in a pack

I like to travel long distances

I live in the Atlantic and Pacific Oceans

I eat fish, crustaceans, jellyfish, crabs, worms, and

octopus

I can live up to a hundred years

Sponge head cat shark

Hello I'm a sponge head cat shark

I live in the Pacific Ocean

I can be up to 51.4 centimeters long

I like deep water

Star spotted smooth hound

Hello I'm a star spotted smooth

hound

I like sand and mud

Boys can live up to nine years

Girls can live up to seventeen years

Girls can be up to ninety-seven centimeters long

Boys can be up to ninety-two centimeters long

I live in the Indian and Pacific Oceans

Starry smooth hound

Hello I'm a starry smooth hound

I like sand and gravel

I live in the Atlantic Ocean

I live in the Black and Mediterranean Seas

I eat crab, lobster, and fish

I can weigh up to 4.8 kilograms

I can be up to 140 centimeters long

Stethacanthus

hello I'm Stethacanthus

I have a dorsal fin that looks

like an anvil

I could be up to two meters long

I lived three hundred and sixty million years ago

I ate fish, crustaceans, and cephalopods

Straight tooth weasel shark

Hello I'm a straight tooth weasel shark

I'm hunted for food

I live in the Pacific Ocean

I like warm water

I can be up to ninety-two centimeters long

Straitolmia

Hello I'm a Straitolmia

I lived 10.3 million years ago

I liked water with very little salt in it

I lived all over the world

I could be up to three hundred fifty centimeters long

Swell shark

Hello I'm a swell shark

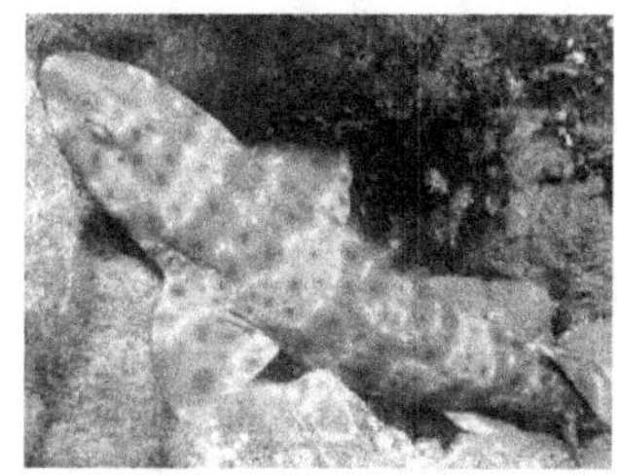

I live in the coastal waters between California and Chile

I eat fish and crustaceans

I can be up to one meter long

I can swell up to twice my normal size if I get scared

I'm awake at night

I'm not an adult until I'm twenty

I'm threatened

Taiwan angel shark

Hello I'm a Taiwan angel shark

I can be up to two meters long

I like sand

I'm endangered

I live in the Pacific Ocean

Taiwan gulper shark

Hello I'm a Taiwan gulper shark

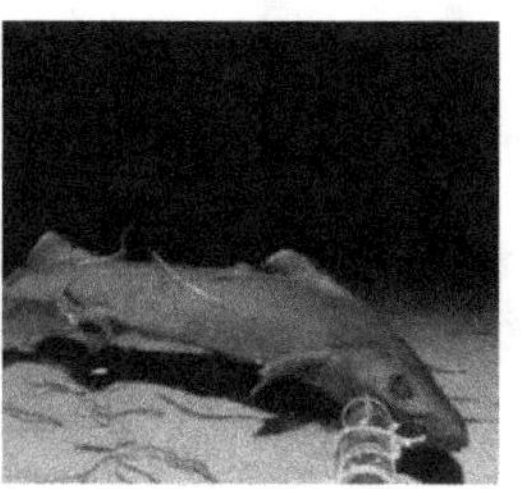

I'm almost threatened

I can be up to 5.6 feet long

I like deep water

I eat lobster, squid, and fish

I'm hunted for oil

Taiwan saddled shark

Hello I'm a Taiwan saddled shark

I can be up to 1.3 feet long

I live in the Pacific Ocean

I'm not a threat to people

Tasselled wobbegong

Hello I'm a tasselled wobbegong

I bite divers who step on me

I'm hunted for leather

I'm almost threatened

I like coral reefs

I live in the Pacific Ocean

I'm awake at night

I like caves

I can be up to twelve feet long

I eat fish who enter my cave

Tawny nurse shark

Hello I'm a tawny nurse shark

I'm hunted as food, fish food, leather, and oil

I can be up to ten feet long

I do well in captivity

I live in the Pacific and Indian Oceans

I like sandy areas, coral reefs, and lagoons

I eat invertebrates, snakes, and fish

I like to explore

Thresher shark

Hello I'm a thresher shark

I cut my food up with my tail

I'm fast

I live in the Pacific Ocean

I eat schooling fish, squid, and cuttlefish

I like to live alone

I can live over twenty years

I'm hunted by people

I'm vulnerable

Tiger cat shark

Hello I'm a tiger cat shark

I eat fish and crustaceans

I can be up to forty-five centimeters long

I live in the Atlantic Ocean

Tiger Shark

Hello I'm a Tiger Shark

I have stripes

I'm one of the largest sharks in the world

I like warm waters

I eat fish, mollusk, crustaceans, birds, mammals, and other smaller sharks

I like to hunt at night

I like to live alone

I can live to be twenty-seven years old

I'm almost threatened

Tope shark

Hello I'm a tope shark

I can live up to sixty years

Adults and children live in two separate groups

Males and Females also live in two separate groups

I'm vulnerable

I live in shallow water in summer

I live in deep water in winter

I live in the Atlantic, Indian, and Pacific Oceans

I eat fish

Tropical saw shark

Hello I'm a tropical saw shark

I live in the Pacific Ocean

I can be up to eighty-five centimeters long

I can have up to eighty-four rows of teeth

I like warm water

Velvet cat shark

Hello I'm a Velvet cat shark

I live near Indonesia

I live in the Pacific Ocean

I can be up to thirty-six centimeters long

I'm awake at night

I sleep in a group during the day

Viper shark

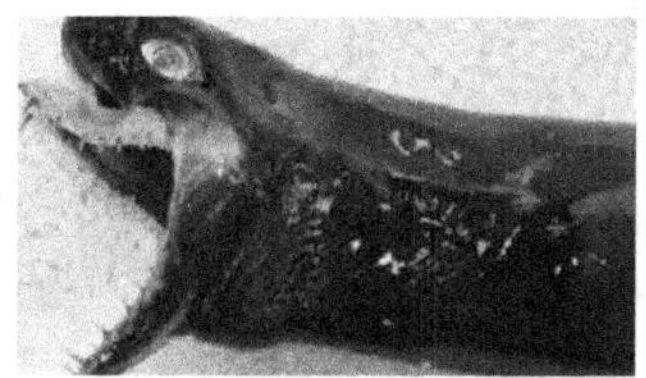

Hello I'm the Viper Shark

I live in the Pacific Ocean

I can glow

I eat fish

I can be up to fifty-three centimeters long

Girls are bigger than boys

Whale shark

Hello I'm a whale

shark

I can be up to twenty meters long

I can have up to three hundred fifty rows of teeth

I live all over the world

I eat fish, krill, crab, jelly fish, plankton and squid

I can live alone or in a group

I let humans near me

I am vulnerable

Whiskery shark

Hello I'm a whiskery shark

I eat octopus, other cephalopods, fish, lobster, worms, and seagrass

I like kelp and rocks

I can live up to fifteen years

I can be up to one hundred sixty centimeters long

I have three eyelids on each side of my head

I live in the Indian Ocean

White bodied cat shark

Hello I'm a white bodied cat shark

I can be up to 59.6 centimeters long

I live in the Pacific Ocean

I like sea mounts and deep water

White cheek shark

Hello I'm a white cheek shark

I like coral reefs and shallow water

I live in the Indo-Pacific

I can be up to 100.7 centimeters long

White fin hammer head

Hello I'm a white fin hammer head

I like warm water

I live near Africa

I eat fish, rays, lobster, shark, and cephalopods

I have to eat two percent of my body weight everyday

I hunt in a group

I can grow up to nine feet long

If a boy loves a girl, he bites her pectoral fin

I'm endangered

White fin tope shark

Hello I'm a white fin tope shark

I have not been seen in fifty years

I'm endangered

I live in the Pacific Ocean

I can be up to ninety-six centimeters long

White ghost cat shark

Hello I'm a white ghost cat shark

I live in the Atlantic Ocean

I like deep water

I can be up to fifty-four centimeters long

White spotted bull head shark

Hello I'm a white spotted bull

head shark

I like warm deep water

I eat crab

I live in the Indian Ocean

I can be up to sixty-four centimeters long

White spotted izak

Hello I'm a white spotted izak

I'm also called an African spotted cat shark

I live in the Indian Ocean

I eat fish, crustaceans, and cephalopods

I'm endangered

As a baby I like deep water

White tip weasel shark

Hello I'm a white tip weasel shark

I live in the Indian Ocean

I like warm shallow water

I can be up to ninety-six centimeters long

Wing head shark

Hello I'm a wing head shark

I live in the Indo-Pacific and the Persian Gulf

I eat fish, crustaceans, and cephalopods

I can have up to thirty rows of teeth

I can live up to twenty-one years

I'm hunted for my meat

I'm endangered

I can be up to one hundred ninety centimeters long

Wobbegong

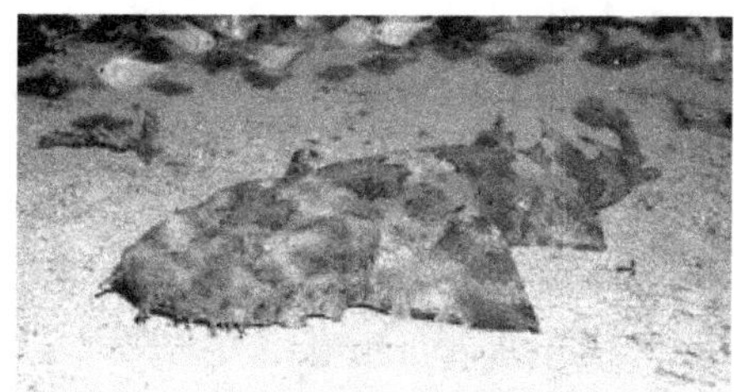

Hello I'm a

wobbegong

I live in the Indian ocean

Girls can be up to 3.2 meters long

Boys can be up to 1.8 meters long

I eat octopus, crab, and sea bass

That swims close to my mouth

As a new born baby I'm twenty-one centimeters long

I will bite anything that steps on me

I'm almost threatened

Xenacanthus

Hello I'm Xenacanthus

I lived in fresh water

I lived two hundred and two million years ago

Zebra bull head shark

Hello I'm a zebra bull head shark

I live in the Pacific Ocean

I can be up to 1.25 meters long

I eat invertebrates, fish, shell fish and mollusk

Zebra shark

Hello I'm a zebra shark

As a baby I have stripes

As an adult I have spots

I live in the coral reefs of

The red sea, the Indian ocean and the Pacific Ocean

I'm awake at night

I'm endangered

Works Cited

www.sharks-world.com

www.google.com/images

www.prehistoric-wildlife.com/species/m/mongolepis.html

www.nationalgeographic.com/science/phenomena/2013/02/26/buzz saw-jaw-helicoprion-was-a-freaky-ratfish/

www.thoughtco.com/history-of-otodus-1093691

www.prehistoric-wildlife.com/species/f/falcatus.html

www.newdinosaurs.com/edestus/

www.britannica.com/animal/Cladoselache

www.sharkwater.com/shark-database/sharks/viper-dogfish/

oceana.org/marine-life/sharks-rays/zebra-shark

www.mcsuk.org/30species/angular-roughshark

www.earthtouchnews.com/oceans/sharks/get-the-facts-on-scotlands-strange-sofa-shark/

www.montereybayaquarium.org/animal-guide/fishes/swell-shark

www.britannica.com/animal/pocket-shark

www.floridamuseum.ufl.edu/discover-fish/species-profiles/isistius-brasiliensis/

animals.mom.me/unusual-lake-nicaragua-shark-7782.html

www.britannica.com/animal/Greenland-shark

www.sharksavers.org/en/education/biology/different-types-of-sharks/saw-sharks/

oceana.org/marine-life/sharks-rays/frilled-shark

www.britannica.com/animal/cat-shark

en.wikipedia.org/wiki/Thresher_shark#Distribution_and_habitat

https://marinebio.org/species/spotted-wobbegong-sharks/orectolobus-maculatus/

www.prehistoric-wildlife.com/species/p/polymerolepis.html

en.wikipedia.org/wiki/Elegestolepis

www.prehistoric-wildlife.com/species/o/orthacanthus.html

www.floridamuseum.ufl.edu/discover-fish/species-profiles/carcharhinus-acronotus/

www.montereybayaquarium.org/animals-and-exhibits/animal-guide/fishes/blacktip-reef-shark?gclid=CjwKCAjw5_DsBRBPEiwAIEDRW4oRI57Mrgh6WhVaBpKYGopcmbW62CWK1YmhpdPMaJQA3A1TX5h4AhoCCqcQAvD_BwE

www.nationalgeographic.com/animals/fish/b/blacktip-shark/

www.sharks.org/brown-shyshark-haploblepharus-fuscus

en.wikipedia.org/wiki/Copper_shark

www.sharksider.com/caribbean-reef-shark/

www.floridamuseum.ufl.edu/discover-fish/species-profiles/carcharhinus-amblyrhynchos/

www.floridamuseum.ufl.edu/discover-fish/species-profiles/carcharhinus-obscurus/

www.floridamuseum.ufl.edu/discover-fish/species-profiles/carcharhinus-galapagensis/

marinebio.org/species/leopard-sharks/triakis-semifasciata/

www.floridamuseum.ufl.edu/discover-fish/species-profiles/carcharhinus-longimanus/

www.nationalgeographic.com/animals/fish/s/sand-tiger-shark/

www.sharks.org/pyjama-shark-poroderma-africanum

www.floridamuseum.ufl.edu/discover-fish/species-profiles/carcharhinus-falciformis/

www.floridamuseum.ufl.edu/discover-fish/species-profiles/carcharhinus-brevipinna/

www.floridamuseum.ufl.edu/discover-fish/species-profiles/carcharhinus-albimarginatus/

marinebio.org/species/horn-sharks/heterodontus-francisci/

www.britannica.com/animal/angel-shark-fish-genus

www.sharks.org/smoothhound-mustelus-mustelus

www.sharkwater.com/shark-database/sharks/sharptooth-lemon-shark/

www.sharks.org/kitefin-shark-dalatias-licha

oceana.org/marine-life/sharks-rays/scalloped-hammerhead-shark

oceana.org/marine-life/sharks-rays/smooth-hammerhead-shark

www.floridamuseum.ufl.edu/discover-fish/species-profiles/lamna-ditropis/

oceana.org/marine-life/sharks-rays/porbeagle-shark

www.sharks.org/crocodile-shark-pseudocarcharias-kamoharai

www.floridamuseum.ufl.edu/discover-fish/species-profiles/hexanchus-griseus/

www.floridamuseum.ufl.edu/discover-fish/species-profiles/notorynchus-cepedianus/

www.floridamuseum.ufl.edu/discover-fish/species-profiles/heptranchias-perlo/

www.sharks.org/bluegrey-carpetshark-geteroscyllium-colcloughi

www.floridamuseum.ufl.edu/discover-fish/species-profiles/ginglymostoma-cirratum/

www.sharksavers.org/en/education/biology/different-types-of-sharks/cow-sharks/

www.floridamuseum.ufl.edu/discover-fish/species-profiles/echinorhinus-brucus/

www.sharkwater.com/shark-database/sharks/great-lanternshark/

www.sdnhm.org/oceanoasis/fieldguide/carcharhinus.html

www.floridamuseum.ufl.edu/discover-fish/species-profiles/carcharhinus-plumbeus/

www.floridamuseum.ufl.edu/discover-fish/species-profiles/negaprion-acutidens/

www.floridamuseum.ufl.edu/discover-fish/species-profiles/nebrius-ferrugineus/

www.floridamuseum.ufl.edu/discover-fish/species-profiles/chiloscyllium-plagiosum/

www.floridamuseum.ufl.edu/discover-fish/species-profiles/hemiscyllium-ocellatum/

www.sharks.org/pygmy-shark-euprotomicrus-bispinatus

www.sharks.org/gulper-shark-centrophorus-granulosus

marinebio.org/species/pacific-sleeper-sharks/somniosus-pacificus/

www.sci-news.com/paleontology/galagadon-nordquistae-06835.html

www.floridamuseum.ufl.edu/discover-fish/species-profiles/heterodontus-portusjacksoni/

australianmuseum.net.au/learn/animals/fishes/prickly-shark-echinorhinus-cookei-pietschmann-1928/

marinesanctuary.org/blog/spiny-dogfish-habitat-management/?gclid=Cj0KCQjw6KrtBRDLARIsAKzvQIFNKDJcS8iXmKjY0yclTdtw1BWBEkczpaN-16V-8-3btdvWYreshFEaAlmOEALw_wcB

en.wikipedia.org/wiki/White_ghost_catshark

www.sharkwater.com/shark-database/sharks/small-eye-catshark/

www.sharkwater.com/shark-database/sharks/iceland-catshark/

www.prehistoric-wildlife.com/species/p/ptychodus.html

en.wikipedia.org/wiki/Acanthodes

www.globalwildlife.org/pondicherry-shark/

www.sharkwater.com/shark-database/sharks/ganges-shark/

en.wikipedia.org/wiki/River_shark

www.sharkwater.com/shark-database/sharks/northern-river-shark/

www.sharkwater.com/shark-database/sharks/dagger-nose-shark/

www.edgeofexistence.org/species/natal-shyshark/

www.scientificamerican.com/gallery/slowly-evolving-elephant-shark-offers-clues-about-why-some-fishes-have-no-bones/

www.sharkwater.com/shark-database/sharks/spear-tooth-shark/

en.wikipedia.org/wiki/Australian_ghostshark

en.wikipedia.org/wiki/Australian_marbled_catshark

www.sharkwater.com/shark-database/sharks/african-dwarf-sawshark/

www.sharkwater.com/shark-database/sharks/angular-angelshark/

en.wikipedia.org/wiki/Balloon_shark

www.bluezooaquatics.com/productDetail.asp?did=1&pid=234&cid=36

en.wikipedia.org/wiki/Coral_catshark

www.sharkwater.com/shark-database/sharks/arabian-carpetshark/

www.sharkwater.com/shark-database/sharks/argentine-angelshark/

www.shark.ch/Database/Search/species.html?sh_id=1058

www.floridamuseum.ufl.edu/discover-fish/species-profiles/paragaleus-pectoralis/

www.sharkwater.com/shark-database/sharks/australian-angelshark/

www.sharkwater.com/shark-database/sharks/australian-black-spotted-catshark/

www.sharkwater.com/shark-database/sharks/australian-weasel-shark/

www.floridamuseum.ufl.edu/discover-fish/species-profiles/cephaloscyllium-laticeps/

www.sharksider.com/zebra-bullhead-shark/

en.wikipedia.org/wiki/Eosqualiolus

www.sharkwater.com/shark-database/sharks/banded-houndshark/

www.prehistoric-wildlife.com/species/b/bandringa.html

en.wikipedia.org/wiki/Barbelthroat_carpetshark

www.sharkwater.com/shark-database/sharks/beige-catshark/

www.sharkwater.com/shark-database/sharks/winghead-shark/

www.sharkwater.com/shark-database/sharks/bigeye-sand-tiger/

en.wikipedia.org/wiki/Bigeye_thresher#Taxonomy_and_phylogeny

www.sharkwater.com/shark-database/sharks/big-head-catshark/

www.sharkwater.com/shark-database/sharks/bird-beak-dogfish/

en.wikipedia.org/wiki/Blackfin_gulper_shark

www.sharkwater.com/shark-database/sharks/black-gill-catshark/

en.wikipedia.org/wiki/Black_roughscale_catshark

www.sharkwater.com/shark-database/sharks/blind-shark/

www.sharkwater.com/shark-database/sharks/blotchy-swellshark/

www.fishbase.se/summary/5902

www.floridamuseum.ufl.edu/discover-fish/species-profiles/sphyrna-tiburo/

www.sharkwater.com/shark-database/sharks/borneo-shark/

en.wikipedia.org/wiki/Brachaelurus

www.sharkwater.com/shark-database/sharks/bristly-catshark/

www.sharkwater.com/shark-database/sharks/broad-banded-lanternsahrk/

www.sharkwater.com/shark-database/sharks/broad-gill-catshark/

www.sharkwater.com/shark-database/sharks/broad-mouth-catshark/

www.sharkwater.com/shark-database/sharks/broad-nose-catshark/

www.sharksavers.org/en/education/biology/different-types-of-sharks/bullhead-sharks/

bie.ala.org.au/species/urn:lsid:biodiversity.org.au:afd.taxon:5f9a22a5-bb6f-4fb5-9662-b1404854258a

www.sharksider.com/burmese-bamboo-shark/

www.sharkwater.com/shark-database/sharks/campeche-catshark/

www.sharkwater.com/shark-database/sharks/caribbean-lanternshark/

www.sharksider.com/caribbean-roughshark/

marinebio.org/species/carolina-hammerhead-sharks/sphyrna-gilberti/

www.sharkwater.com/shark-database/sharks/chilean-angelshark/

www.sharkwater.com/shark-database/sharks/cloudy-catshark/

australianmuseum.net.au/learn/animals/fishes/cobbler-wobbegong-sutorectus-tentaculatus/

bie.ala.org.au/species/urn:lsid:biodiversity.org.au:afd.taxon:3f26f5d
5-f8fe-42ee-a26c-7c4510c0865d

www.sharkwater.com/shark-database/sharks/comb-tooth-
lanternshark/

www.floridamuseum.ufl.edu/florida-vertebrate-
fossils/species/carcharodon-hastalis

www.sharksider.com/crested-bullhead-shark/

www.sharkwater.com/shark-database/sharks/dark-shyshark/

www.sharkwater.com/shark-database/sharks/deep-water-catshark/

www.sharkwater.com/shark-database/sharks/eastern-angelshark/

www.sharkwater.com/shark-database/sharks/deep-water-sicklefin-
houndshark/

www.sharkwater.com/shark-database/sharks/dusky-smooth-hound/

en.wikipedia.org/wiki/Dumb_gulper_shark

ocean.si.edu/ocean-life/sharks-rays/dwarf-lantern-shark

www.elasmodiver.com/Dwarf%20Ornate%20Wobbegong%20Shar
k.htm

www.sharkwater.com/shark-database/sharks/dwarf-sawtail-
catshark/

www.sharkwater.com/shark-database/sharks/dwarf-spotted-
wobbegong/

en.wikipedia.org/wiki/Fedorov%27s_catshark

www.floridamuseum.ufl.edu/discover-fish/species-
profiles/parmaturus-xaniurus/

www.sharkwater.com/shark-database/sharks/flaccid-catshark/

www.sharkwater.com/shark-database/sharks/flat-head-catshark/

www.sharkwater.com/shark-database/sharks/floral-banded-
wobbegong/

en.wikipedia.org/wiki/Fringefin_lanternshark

www.sharkwater.com/shark-database/sharks/frog-shark/

www.sharkwater.com/shark-database/sharks/galapagos-bullhead-
shark/

en.wikipedia.org/wiki/Galeus

www.sharkwater.com/shark-database/sharks/ginger-carpetshark/

www.sharkwater.com/shark-database/sharks/grey-bamboo-shark/

en.wikipedia.org/wiki/Gulf_wobbegong

en.wikipedia.org/wiki/Gummy_shark

marinebio.org/species/halmahera-epaulette-sharks/hemiscyllium-halmahera/

www.sharkwater.com/shark-database/sharks/hasselts-bamboo-shark/

en.wikipedia.org/wiki/Hemipristis_serra

www.sharkwater.com/shark-database/sharks/hoary-catshark/

www.sharkwater.com/shark-database/sharks/hooded-carpet-shark/

www.sharkwater.com/shark-database/sharks/hooktooth-shark/

www.sharkwater.com/shark-database/sharks/humpback-catshark/

www.sharkwater.com/shark-database/sharks/big-eye-houndshark/

en.wikipedia.org/wiki/Indonesian_houndshark

www.sharkwater.com/shark-database/sharks/indonesian-speckled-carpet-shark/

planetsharkdivers.com/indonesian-wobbegong/

www.sharkwater.com/shark-database/sharks/izak-catshark/

www.sharkwater.com/shark-database/sharks/japanese-angelshark/

en.wikipedia.org/wiki/Japanese_bullhead_shark

www.sharkwater.com/shark-database/sharks/japanese-catshark/

www.sharksider.com/japanese-sawshark/

en.wikipedia.org/wiki/Japanese_topeshark

www.sharksider.com/japanese-wobbegong/

www.sharkwater.com/shark-database/sharks/lanas-sawshark/

en.wikipedia.org/wiki/Largetooth_cookiecutter_shark

www.sharksider.com/leafscale-gulper-shark/

www.floridamuseum.ufl.edu/discover-fish/species-profiles/poroderma-pantherinum/

www.sharkwater.com/shark-database/sharks/leopard-epaulette-shark/

www.sharkwater.com/shark-database/sharks/little-gulper-shark/

en.wikipedia.org/wiki/Little_sleeper_shark

www.sharkwater.com/shark-database/sharks/long-head-catshark/

en.wikipedia.org/wiki/Longnose_catshark

www.sharkwater.com/shark-database/sharks/long-nose-sawshark/

en.wikipedia.org/wiki/Lost_shark

planetsharkdivers.com/lowfin-gulper-shark/

www.sharkwater.com/shark-database/sharks/mcmillans-catshark/

www.sharkwater.com/shark-database/sharks/mexican-horn-shark/

www.sharkwater.com/shark-database/sharks/mosaic-gulper-shark/

www.sharkwater.com/shark-database/sharks/mouse-catshark/

www.sharkwater.com/shark-database/sharks/narrow-mouthed-catshark/

www.sharkwater.com/shark-database/sharks/narrow-tail-catshark/

www.floridamuseum.ufl.edu/discover-fish/species-profiles/parascyllium-variolatum/

en.wikipedia.org/wiki/Negaprion_eurybathrodon

www.sharkwater.com/shark-database/sharks/northern-wobbegong/

planetsharkdivers.com/ocellated-angelshark/

www.sharkwater.com/shark-database/sharks/oman-bullhead-shark/

en.wikipedia.org/wiki/Orectolobus_hutchinsi

en.wikipedia.org/wiki/Orectolobus_reticulatus

www.sharkwater.com/shark-database/sharks/ornate-wobbegong/

www.sharkwater.com/shark-database/sharks/pacific-angelshark/

www.sharkwater.com/shark-database/sharks/whitetip-weasel-shark/

www.edgeofexistence.org/species/whitespotted-izak/

www.sharkwater.com/shark-database/sharks/white-spotted-bullhead-shark/

www.sharkwater.com/shark-database/sharks/whitefin-topeshark/

www.sharksider.com/facts-know-whitefin-hammerhead-shark%E2%80%A8/

www.sharkwater.com/shark-database/sharks/whitecheek-shark/

www.sharkwater.com/shark-database/sharks/pale-catshark/

www.sharkwater.com/shark-database/sharks/panama-ghost-catshark/

www.sharkwater.com/shark-database/sharks/papuan-epaulette-shark/

www.floridamuseum.ufl.edu/discover-fish/species-profiles/alopias-pelagicus/

fishesofaustralia.net.au/home/species/1962

en.wikipedia.org/wiki/Blacktip_tope

www.sharkwater.com/shark-database/sharks/pinocchio-catshark/

www.sharkwater.com/shark-database/sharks/plunkets-shark/

en.wikipedia.org/wiki/Pristiophorus_striatus

www.floridamuseum.ufl.edu/discover-fish/species-profiles/haploblepharus-edwardsii/

www.sharkwater.com/shark-database/sharks/pygmy-ribbontail-catshark/

www.sharkwater.com/shark-database/sharks/quagga-catshark/

www.sharkwater.com/shark-database/sharks/red-spotted-catshark/

www.sharkwater.com/shark-database/sharks/reticulated-swellshark/

www.sharkwater.com/shark-database/sharks/rough-skin-catshark/

www.sharkwater.com/shark-database/sharks/rusty-carpetshark/

www.sharkwater.com/shark-database/sharks/saddle-carpetshark/

www.sharkwater.com/shark-database/sharks/salamander-catshark/

www.sharkwater.com/shark-database/sharks/saldanha-catshark/

planetsharkdivers.com/sand-devil-or-atlantic-angel-shark/

www.sharksider.com/sawback-angelshark/

www.sharkwater.com/shark-database/sharks/scalloped-bonnethead/

www.sharkwater.com/shark-database/sharks/school-shark/

www.sharkwater.com/shark-database/sharks/scoop-head-hammerhead/

www.sharkwater.com/shark-database/sharks/sharptooth-houndshark/

www.sharkwater.com/shark-database/sharks/green-lanternshark/

www.sharksider.com/shortfin-mako-shark/

www.sharkwater.com/shark-database/sharks/short-nose-demon-catshark/

www.sharkwater.com/shark-database/sharks/short-nose-sawshark/

www.sharkwater.com/shark-database/sharks/short-tail-lanternshark/

www.sharkwater.com/shark-database/sharks/short-tail-nurse-shark/

www.sharkwater.com/shark-database/sharks/sickle-fin-smooth-hound/

www.sharkwater.com/shark-database/sharks/sicklefin-weasel-shark/

www.sharkwater.com/shark-database/sharks/six-gill-sawshark/

www.sharkwater.com/shark-database/sharks/slender-bamboo-shark/

www.sharkwater.com/shark-database/sharks/slender-weasel-shark/

www.sharkwater.com/shark-database/sharks/slit-eye-shark/

www.sharkwater.com/shark-database/sharks/small-belly-catshark/

www.sharkwater.com/shark-database/sharks/small-dorsal-catshark/

www.floridamuseum.ufl.edu/discover-fish/species-profiles/sphyrna-tudes/

www.sharkwater.com/shark-database/sharks/small-eye-pygmy-shark/

www.sharkwater.com/shark-database/sharks/small-fin-catshark/

www.sharkwater.com/shark-database/sharks/small-fin-gulper-shark/

en.wikipedia.org/wiki/Smalltooth_sand_tiger

www.fossilguy.com/gallery/vert/fish-shark/hemipristis/hemipristis.htm

www.edgeofexistence.org/species/tope-shark/

www.sharkwater.com/shark-database/sharks/velvet-catshark/

www.sharkwater.com/shark-database/sharks/south-china-catshark/

planetsharkdivers.com/south-china-cookiecutter-shark/

animals.fandom.com/wiki/Southern_African_Frilled_Shark

www.sharkwater.com/shark-database/sharks/southern-sleeper-shark/

www.sharkwater.com/shark-database/sharks/borneo-catshark/

www.sharkwater.com/shark-database/sharks/white-bodied-catshark/

www.sharkwater.com/shark-database/sharks/whiskery-shark/

www.sharkwater.com/shark-database/sharks/tropical-sawshark/

www.sharkwater.com/shark-database/sharks/speckled-carpet-shark/

www.sharkwater.com/shark-database/sharks/spined-pygmy-shark/

www.sharkwater.com/shark-database/sharks/sponge-head-catshark/

www.sharkwater.com/shark-database/sharks/star-spotted-smooth-hound/

www.sharkwater.com/shark-database/sharks/starry-smooth-hound/

www.sharkwater.com/shark-database/sharks/straight-tooth-weasel-shark/

en.wikipedia.org/wiki/Striatolamia

www.sharkwater.com/shark-database/sharks/taiwan-angelshark/

planetsharkdivers.com/taiwan-gulper-shark/

planetsharkdivers.com/taiwan-saddled-carpetshark/

www.floridamuseum.ufl.edu/discover-fish/species-profiles/eucrossorhinus-dasypogon/

www.sharkwater.com/shark-database/sharks/tiger-catshark/